STORIES OF JESUS

HAZELD QUIRK

Mary talks to Elizabeth at Nazareth

Stories of

Jesus

*

Margaret Bullough

Illustrated by T. D. Grice

LONDON: THE EPWORTH PRESS

Published by
THE EPWORTH PRESS
(FRANK H. CUMBERS)
25-35 City Road, London, E.C.1.

New York . *Toronto*

Melbourne . *Cape Town*

Printed in Great Britain by
A. BROWN & SONS, LTD.
Hull and London.

CONTENTS

FOREWORD ABOUT THE AUTHOR

SOME of you girls and boys will be just eight, and some twelve, or even twelve plus.

So some of you may be, I am sure you all *will* be, happy up to Chapter VIII.

But though VIII stands for 8, you who are 8 may find VIII perhaps a little bit difficult to understand. If so, give it a miss, just now; later on it will be 'just so'.

And the same with Chapter XIII. Just say to yourself: 'XIII stands for 13, so when I'm 13 I'll be equal to it'.

And now 'one word more' ('one' sometimes runs on into 100); one word about the author of the *Stories of Jesus*. I saw her first when she was twelve, and ever since we have been friends, and we are great friends still. I do know she has always loved stories about Jesus, and loved telling the 'stories of Jesus'; her own little children loved to hear these stories, so I know she is a really good story-teller.

'And who are you?' you ask. Just think of me as

THE PARTNER.

CHAPTER I

MARY AND ELIZABETH

LONG, long ago, in the beautiful little town of Nazareth across the sea, there lived a simple country girl called Mary.

Nazareth was a radiant place. Its white houses, nestling amongst groups of fine trees, shone in the sun. It was gay with many coloured flowers and always looked wonderfully fresh, clean, and bright.

Mary's home, one of these white houses, was built on the upper slope of a hill, so she had a fine view of the lovely surrounding country.

Below she could see a winding river, a shining blue lake, beautifully wooded hills and mountains and even, far away, a glimpse of the blue sea.

You may be surprised to hear that Mary often enjoyed this lovely view from the housetop. You would think it very strange to see anyone seated on the housetop in this country, wouldn't you? You would wonder how they had got there and would be afraid they would fall off and kill themselves.

But in that country of Palestine, the houses were mostly only one storey high and had a flat roof. This was used as an open-air room, a kind of sun-parlour, in summer time. Many people slept on the roof in the summer because it was so hot. If we did that we should sometimes be caught in a shower of rain. But in Palestine most of the rain falls in the winter time. You could sleep outside in peace after May was out until the beginning of November.

But if you lived in that country you would not sleep in beds. You would spread out on the roof, if you were sleeping there, a mat or rug and lie down on that. You would be quite warm in that climate.

Perhaps you will say, 'What if I rolled off the roof in my sleep?' There would be no danger of that because a balustrade—a low wall or railing—would run all round, so you would be quite safe.

In the morning when you got up, you would roll up your rug and put it away. So your bed-making would be very easy, wouldn't it?

But now you ask, 'How should I get up on to the roof?'

Well, if you went round the side of the house you would find a flight of stone steps running up the wall. You would reach the roof by these steps.

Now Mary liked sitting on the roof enjoying the cool fresh air in the summer time. And she sometimes sat there with her cousin Elizabeth when she came on a visit to Mary's home. She was much older than Mary and had been married quite a long time. But they were very great friends and, as all friends do, they told all their secrets to one another.

One day the two cousins were sitting side by side on their rugs in their usual way on the roof, which looked quite pretty decorated with flowers. A vine trailed its green leaves over the balustrade and clusters of ripe fruit hung temptingly near.

Elizabeth was busy with the kind of embroidery the women of that country do so cleverly. Skeins of coloured silks lay on the rug beside her.

Mary's hands lay idly in her lap. She was gazing out, very contentedly, over the beautiful country.

Elizabeth lifted her eyes to Mary's face and said: 'You do look happy, Mary.'

'Yes, I feel happy,' answered Mary. 'Everything seems so lovely today. Look how the lake sparkles as though the stars had fallen into it,' and she pointed to the Sea of Galilee below. 'And just look at the glistening snowy head of Mount Hermon towering into the very heavens. And can you see, Elizabeth, where that far glimmer of shining sea meets those pearly clouds on the horizon? Is it not like fairyland?'

'Yes, it is all very lovely, I know,' answered Elizabeth, 'but I am afraid I cannot feel quite so happy as you do, Mary.'

'I know, dear,' said Mary kindly, 'I am so sorry you have that big disappointment in your life. But don't give up hope. You may yet have your heart's desire, Elizabeth.'

'Yes,' answered Elizabeth, 'we pray about it every day. Perhaps God will yet hear and answer us.'

'God always hears our prayers, dear,' said Mary, 'and if it is for the best, He grants us our desire. I do hope He will grant yours, Elizabeth.'

'Thank you, Mary,' replied Elizabeth, looking gratefully at her cousin.

In a few days Elizabeth returned to her own home.

When the two cousins said goodbye they little dreamed what wonderful news they would very soon have to tell each other.

MARY

Mary is good as she is gay,
She sings at work, she sings at play,
Like a sweet thrush in a green tree
So Mary sings, O, merrily.

Fair angels in their heavenly bowers
Hear Mary singing at all hours,
They strike their harps when Mary sings,
The harmony through Heaven rings.

Mary is gay as she is good,
She makes, as all good people should,
A little heaven where she lives,
She gives her all, herself she gives.

Chapter II

MARY'S VISION

MARY's home was a humble one. Her parents were not well-to-do, so they could not afford to have a servant. Every day Mary was very busy helping her mother to do the housework.

She was a happy girl and went about the house singing like a bird as she helped to wash the clothes, clean the house, and bake the bread.

Often you would have found her sitting at her spinning wheel. She would be spinning woollen and flax fibre into thread. This thread would then be woven into linen and woollen cloth (linsey-woolsey) for garments, sheets, curtains and many other articles. Many of the women sold some of the things they had made and probably Mary would do the same. But she would help to make clothes and household linen for the home and her people first.

One day she sat spinning all by herself at her wheel, using her fingers to hold the fibre and her foot to turn the wheel.

She was singing softly, to the gentle hum of the wheel, a psalm she had heard on the

Sabbath in the synagogue, as the church was called. Suddenly God gave her a wonderful vision.

She saw an angel sent from Heaven standing in the room. He was clothed in shining white garments, and he said: 'Oh Mary, you are a greatly favoured woman—the Lord is with you!'

Now Mary was terrified and wondered what these words of the angel could possibly mean.

But the angel said to her: 'Do not be afraid, Mary, God is very pleased with you.'

Then the angel told her that God was about to give her a very great honour. He had chosen her out of all the women of the world to be the mother of the Holy One He had promised for so long to send from Heaven.

And the angel said: 'You must call His name Jesus.'

Mary answered: 'Let God do with me whatever pleases Him.'

Then the angel said: 'Your cousin, Elizabeth, will soon have her heart's desire. A little baby boy is being sent to her.' Then the angel left her.

As soon as he was gone, Mary said to herself: 'I must go at once and tell Elizabeth about this.' So she got ready and went as quickly as she could to her cousin's house.

What a story she had to tell her! She was

full of joy and said: 'I do thank God for the wonderful thing that has happened to me. How happy I am that God has chosen me, a poor country girl, to be the mother of His Son. Everyone who is born into this world, both now and throughout all future time, will call me the happiest and most honoured of women. And oh, Elizabeth, I am indeed happy!'

Elizabeth also was full of joy and said: 'You are indeed, Mary, the most favoured of all women. But I do not feel worthy of a visit from the mother of the Messiah.'

They talked for some time about Mary's great news and then Elizabeth told her cousin about the great happiness that was coming to her also.

Her husband, Zacharias, was a priest. In these days he would be called a clergyman or minister.

When he was praying for the people in the temple he had a vision something like the one Mary had. A shining angel appeared to him and he was afraid.

But the angel said: 'Do not be afraid, Zacharias, God has heard your prayers and Elizabeth's and He will soon send you a little baby boy. You must call his name John. He will make you both very happy and many people will be glad that ever he was born. He

will be a great and a good man. He will teach
people to love God and live good lives and will
show them how to get ready for the coming
of the Holy One God is sending from Heaven.'

You can imagine how much Mary and
Elizabeth had to say to one another and how
much they would help each other in their
preparations for the coming of their little
babies! At last, however, Mary had to return
to her own home, but she had stayed with
her cousin for three months.

I think when Mary got home she would
sing more than ever in her great happiness.
Perhaps she would sing a song something like
this:

MARY'S SONG

O what a happy, happy girl am I!
    What great things God has done,
To make a simple village-girl like me
    The mother of His Son.

An angel from the shining realms above
    On radiant wings did fly
To me, so lowly in my humble home,
    O happy, happy I!

Now all the people in the world will say:
    'O happy, happy maid!
To see the sweet head of that holy Babe
    Upon your bosom laid.'

Chapter III

THE COMING OF THE BABY JESUS

A FEW months after this Mary got married
to a good, kind man called Joseph. He was
a carpenter and had a workshop in Nazareth
and there Mary went to live. She was very
happy living with Joseph because he was so
kind and gentle.

Now their country, called Palestine, had
been conquered by the Romans and was ruled
by the Roman Emperor, Caesar Augustus.

About this time he sent out a command
that everyone must go to their own city or
town and have their names written on a
register so that he could count the number of
people in the country.

Now, although Joseph lived in Nazareth,
his family came from Bethlehem, so he went
there and took Mary with him.

It was a long journey, about eighty miles.
We should not think it long in these days,
because we could take a train and do it in
less than two hours.

But there were no trains or 'buses in those
days. Mary and Joseph had to do most of the
journey on foot. So they travelled as far as

they could each day and rested somewhere for the night, perhaps in an inn or even in some quiet spot by the roadside. At last, after a good many days, they came to Bethlehem.

Mary was very tired, so Joseph began to look round at once for somewhere to rest and sleep.

It was very difficult to find because a great many other people had travelled to Bethlehem for the same purpose and had arrived there before them. They had taken all the bed-rooms and beds, so the only place Joseph and Mary could find for themselves was the stable of the inn. This was a very rough place but they made the best of it.

They ate the food they had with them and then lay down on some of the straw that had been put there for the cows and donkeys.

Then, in this poor place, the most wonderful of all things happened. During the night God sent little baby Jesus down from Heaven to Mary and Joseph.

Of course there was no nice cradle or little cot ready for Him, so Mary had to lay Him in a manger, one of the long boxes from which the animals ate their food.

How strange it seems to us, does it not, that the Son of God should be born in a stable and have a manger for a cradle? Would you not **have** thought **He** would have been born a prince and have lived in a palace? A lot of people thought that would have happened.

But no, that was not God's way. He was sent to poor people and lived all His life with the poor, the simple, and the lowly.

There were very few people in the world who knew of the marvellous thing that had happened that night. But God sent His messengers to tell a few chosen ones.

Some of these were simple shepherds.

In the fields round about Bethlehem large flocks of sheep were kept. After dark, wild animals, especially wolves, prowled about in search of food. No sheep or lamb was safe from them. So the shepherds gathered their sheep together into a fold made of hurdles and stayed out all night to protect them.

The shepherd loved his sheep and after he had gathered them together into the fold and counted them to see that none had strayed away, he would lie down in the doorway or opening of the fold ready, if need be, to fight any fierce wolf that tried to enter the fold to snatch a sheep or lamb. Some shepherds had been known to give their lives to save the sheep in this way. Every sheep had its own name and would come when the shepherd called it. They knew their own shepherd's voice and would follow him as a dog follows its master.

On the night Jesus was born some of these good shepherds were out in the quiet fields around Bethlehem keeping watch over their sheep. In the distance they could see the lights glimmering in the houses of Bethlehem. Then they saw them go out one by one as the people went to bed. It was a moonless night, but overhead the stars were shining, though darkness deepened all around them. Then they talked quietly together and some dropped off into a doze.

But suddenly their eyes were dazzled by a glorious light from Heaven which shone all around them. Then they saw an angel of God standing by them and they were filled with terror and hid their faces.

But the angel said to them: 'Do not be afraid. I have brought you good news of great joy for all the people on earth. A Baby has been born in Bethlehem and He is the Saviour, Christ the Lord. You will find the Babe wrapped in baby-clothes and lying in a manger.'

And suddenly there was with the angel a multitude of angels from Heaven and they all burst out singing very joyfully:

> 'Glory to God in the highest
> And on earth peace,
> Good will towards men.'

When the angels had flown back into Heaven the shepherds said to one another: 'Come, let us go at once to Bethlehem and see this thing that has happened and that God has made known to us.'

So they went with great haste and found the stable and went in. And there they saw Mary and Joseph and the little Baby lying in the manger just as the angel had told them.

And they were filled with wonder about it all and told people about seeing the angels and what they had said about the Baby. And everyone who heard it was greatly amazed.

And Mary listened intently to all the words the shepherds said and ever after remembered them, turning them over and over in her mind.

CHAPTER IV

THE COMING OF THE BABY JESUS
(*continued*)

THE WISE MEN

THERE were some others whom God told about the coming of the Baby Jesus.

In a country called Persia, a long way from Bethlehem, there lived three great and good men. Because they had great knowledge they were called in those days 'Wise Men'. In these days we should call them 'men of science'. These three Wise Men studied many things, but especially the stars. They thought the stars could tell them things by their movements.

Every night these three men went together on to the top of the house and watched the stars, talking about them together.

One night as they were watching they were amazed to see a new star, very large and brilliant, shining in the eastern part of the sky.

Then they all began talking together very eagerly. They thought this wonderful star must mean something very special.

So they looked in their star-book and they found that when that star appeared it meant that a Baby Prince had been born somewhere in the world.

Then they looked at the star again and saw that it was moving slowly across the sky. This was very strange and wonderful, and they said to one another: 'Let us get ready and follow this strange star. Perhaps it will guide us to the place where the Baby Prince has been born.'

When the sun rose the next morning, of course, the star disappeared, but they spent the day getting ready to follow the star when it appeared the next night.

They had noticed the star was moving towards the west. That meant they had to cross a desert. So they got their camels ready and loaded them with water-bottles of leather and food to last them their journey across the sand.

Then, as they were going to pay a visit to a Prince, they bought presents suitable to offer to Him.

When darkness came on they saw with great joy that the star was still in the sky, so they turned their faces to the west and set out on their camels. The star moved along right over their heads and then went on before them.

All through the night the Wise Men followed the star and when morning came and the star could not be seen, they made their camp and rested and slept until darkness once more made the star visible.

So they followed the wonderful star night after night, a great many nights, for they had a long way to go.

At last they found the star had guided them to a large and beautiful city. They were told this city was called Jerusalem and that a king was living there who was the king of the Jews. Jerusalem was the chief city, the capital of the country, and the king's palace was there.

Then they said to one another: 'Surely we shall find the Baby Prince here. He will be the King of the Jews when he grows up and will live in the palace.'

So they went about the city asking people they met if a prince had been born there recently because a star had told them there had been, and had guided them.

Well, of course, no one had heard of a prince being born and everyone thought it very strange and rather upsetting.

At last it came to the ears of the king who was called Herod. He was very troubled and jealous.

'I am the king of the Jews,' he said to himself, 'and *my* son is the prince who will be king after me. But who is this Baby

Prince these Wise Men are talking about, who will be, they say, the King of the Jews instead of my son?'

King Herod knew that for a long time the Jewish people had been expecting God to send Someone called the Christ or the Messiah and that they hoped He would be their King.

Now this was written in the Scriptures, which we call the Old Testament. So he called to him certain men who spent most of their time studying the Scriptures and commanded them to tell him where Christ should be born.

And they said: 'In Bethlehem He will be born; the Scriptures say so. The prophets have written it.'

So then Herod sent for the three Wise Men. And he asked them all about the star and when they had first seen it.

When they had told him everything he said: 'I believe the Baby Prince is in Bethlehem. It is not many miles from this city. You go and search very carefully for Him and when you have found Him bring me word so that I may also go and see Him and pay homage to Him.'

So the Wise Men left the palace and set out for Bethlehem about eight miles away. Then they waited until darkness fell so that they could see the star. When they saw it they rejoiced with exceeding great joy for it was moving and guiding them again to the Baby. The wonderful star went before them till it came and stood over where the young Child was.

Then they went in and saw the Child with Mary, His mother, and they knelt down and paid homage to Him. And opening their treasure-boxes they presented to Him their gifts.

But that night God warned them in a dream not to go back to King Herod to tell him where the Child Jesus was. So they travelled back home another way.

But when Herod found out that the Wise Men had not done what he had commanded them, he was extremely angry. He was determined he would get rid of that Baby Prince. So he called his soldiers and said: 'Go and kill every little boy baby in Bethlehem and in all the country round about it, from two years old and under.'

Then how the poor mothers wept and tried to hide their babies! But the cruel king had no pity. They mourned for a long time and would not be comforted because their little children were dead.

So King Herod thought he had certainly killed the Child Jesus amongst the other little children. But, no, God had taken care of Him.

That same night when He had warned the Wise Men in a dream, Joseph also had a dream in which God said to him: 'Get ready at once and take the young Child and His mother and flee into the land of Egypt, for Herod is a bad man and will seek the young Child to destroy Him.'

So Joseph got up instantly and took Jesus and Mary by night into Egypt and stayed there until he heard that Herod was dead.

Then he set out on the road back to Bethlehem. But hearing on the way that Herod's son was now king in his place and fearing that he might be as wicked as his father, he turned aside and went to live once more in Nazareth.

> The shepherds had an angel,
>   The wise men had a star;
> But what have I, a little child
>   To guide me home from far,
> Where glad stars sing together,
>   And singing angels are?
>
> Those shepherds through the lonely night
>   Sat watching by their sheep,
> Until they saw the heavenly host
>   Who neither tire nor sleep,
> All singing Glory, glory,
>   In festival they keep.

Christ watches me, His little lamb,
  Cares for me day and night,
That I may be His own in Heaven:
  So angels clad in white
Shall sing their Glory, glory,
  For my sake in the height.

Chapter V

THE BOY JESUS

So here at Nazareth their dear little Boy Jesus lived with His father and mother.

His father went on with his work as a carpenter and so earned a living for Mary and Jesus.

Jesus loved to go into His father's workshop and watch him sawing logs of wood and then using chisel and hammer to make doors, wheels, tables and cupboards, ploughs and yokes and lots of other things that people asked Joseph to make for them.

When Jesus was quite little His father let Him help sometimes with a little toy set of tools that he had made Him for His third birthday.

After a time more babies came to the home and Jesus had little brothers and sisters to love and play with. He was their big kind brother. And as His mother could not afford a servant He helped her in every way He could.

But now He is a little boy. He will go to school soon. Every little Jewish boy started to go to school when he was six years old.

Until that time all good Jewish mothers taught their children at home.

So Mary taught Jesus and how she must have loved it: so eager, so quick, so intelligent He must have been.

Until a little Jewish boy or girl was ten years old they were not allowed to learn to read from any book except the Holy Scriptures, the book we call the Old Testament.

So Jesus sat at His mother's knee and learned His letters and then to read little words.

Before He went to bed at night she told Him some of the stories you know, about Joseph and his brothers, Daniel in the lion's den, little Samuel in the Temple, David and Jonathan, and lots more. She told them so beautifully and Jesus loved to listen to her and wouldn't have missed His bedtime story for anything. We know that when He grew up He knew almost every word of the Bible from end to end. And knew so well what it all meant, too. Well, His mother was His first teacher and perhaps His best. We know how good she was.

At last the day came when Jesus went to school. But it was not the kind of school you go to. Jesus would go to the church, or the synagogue as the building was called. His mother was a busy mother, but perhaps she

took Him the first time, or perhaps He went
with some other little boys He played with
near His home.

When He got there He was put into a class
with about twenty other little boys. But you
must not imagine that Jesus sat at a desk as
you do. He sat with the others on a mat on
the floor. They formed a semi-circle and the
master did not stand, but also sat on a mat
in front of them.

He taught them reading and writing and
numbers just as your teacher does. But Jesus
still had more lessons about the Old Testament than about anything else. They had
their reading lessons from it, and Jesus soon
learned to read for Himself the stories His
mother had told Him.

As He got older He went into a higher class
and began to read parts of the Bible that
were more difficult for a young boy than the
stories. But Jesus would love them very
much because they had been written by men
who knew a great deal about God.

God had talked to them in their hearts and
so they knew better than anyone else what
He was really like. They had very different
thoughts about God than many Jesus listened
to at that time.

They said that God's heart was full of love
and kindness, and that He wanted everyone

Jesus alone in the wilderness

to be happy and to learn to be pure and good so that they could live with Him in the Heavenly Home when they left this world.

They said God was very sad when He saw people making themselves miserable and ill by doing wrong. He wanted them to come to Him to be forgiven and made happy again. When they suffered He felt their pain and longed to heal them.

As Jesus read these beautiful words He said to Himself: 'What a lovely God this is!' and He read on eagerly more and more about Him.

He came running home full of joy to tell His mother all about it.

'Oh mother,' He cried, 'God is just like a very kind and loving father. Mother, I shall call God "My Father".'

'God *is* Your Father, my dear Child,' His mother said and she kissed Him very tenderly. Then she thought over again of what the angels had said about Jesus when He was born.

Not long after, Jesus came home and said: 'Mother, we were reading in school today about Someone called the Messiah. Who is the Messiah, mother?'

Then Mary said: 'Your Heavenly Father has promised for a long time to send Someone down from Heaven to tell all the people about Himself.

c

'As you know, dear, most people we know think God very stern, always waiting to punish them whenever they do wrong. This thought of God makes them very miserable.

'But God has told me in my heart that He is sending the Messiah to tell these sad people that He loves them and does not want to hurt them, that He is their Father and they are His children. He will tell them that God wants them to be happy and is full of pity for them when they suffer.'

'Oh yes, mother,' cried the Boy, 'I know My Heavenly Father is like that. Oh mother, how glorious it will be for the Messiah to be able to go about telling all the people such good news. How joyfully I would do it! I feel He is everyone's Father as well as mine; no matter what colour they are, white people, yellow, brown or black people, He is their Father. So they are all brothers and sisters, God's big family.'

Jesus had got more and more excited as He poured out all this into His mother's ears and now He was quite out of breath.

His mother stared at Him: 'Why, sonny,' she said, 'what has put all that into your head?'

'I don't know, mother,' answered the Boy, 'I think it is all here,' and He laid His hand on His breast.

'And you would like to do that wonderful work for your Heavenly Father when you are a man, would you, my son?' asked His mother.

'Oh yes, mother,' He replied, 'more than anything else in all the world!'

'Perhaps you will,' said Mary quietly.

There was silence for a few minutes and then Jesus said: 'Mother, when can I go with you and father to Jerusalem?'

'You must be patient for a little while yet, dear,' she replied. 'I know how very much you long to go but, you know, children are not allowed to go to the festival until they are twelve years of age.'

'Yes, mother, but I shall be twelve next year, shall I not? Then I may go to see our lovely Jerusalem, the Holy City, my Father's own city. Oh mother, how I long to see it! But it is my Father's House, the beautiful Temple that I want to see most of all. I shall be able to kneel and worship Him along with all the other people at the Feast of the Passover, shall I not?

And I do want to talk to the Rabbis, mother, I want them to tell me so much about my Heavenly Father. They have studied the Bible very deeply, have they not? I want to ask them hundreds of questions. Surely those good wise men will be able to tell me all I am longing to know about my Father?'

Well, Jesus had to wait as we all have to do so often, but the next year He got His heart's desire. Every year His parents had been to the festival, called the Feast of the Passover. Thousands of people went from all over the country and from other countries also.

And now the time had come when Jesus could go also. How excited He was!

At last the day came. Mary and Joseph got the water-bottles and food ready to take with them. They also made a bundle of warm cloaks to wrap round them when they camped out at night. Then they set off, along with many others, friends and relatives.

They walked down the slope of the hill from Nazareth into the valley below through which the River Jordan ran south. They travelled for many miles along the banks of this river, camping out every night by the roadside. They made fires to boil water and cook their evening meal. Then they spread their mats and settled down to sleep. It was very jolly for the girls and boys to sleep out in the open-air, wrapped in their warm cloaks.

The next morning they would set out again. The whole journey took them more than a week, for it was a long one.

As they travelled on, Jesus saw all sorts of interesting things. He would often see camels padding along the road carrying men and big loads of one kind or another on their backs. He would see lots of patient-looking donkeys trotting along, always with burdens on their backs. Then He would see a ploughman driving the ox that pulled the plough. They would pass through many villages and He would see barefooted girls going to the village well to draw water. How gracefully they carried their pitchers upon their heads.

As they drew nearer to Jerusalem they were joined by more and more people going to the festival, until there was a great procession of pilgrims all eagerly waiting for the first glimpse of the Holy City.

At last they got to hill country again and began to climb.

Ah, there it is at last, high on the hills, with its gleaming white walls and houses! And look! There on the highest part of the city is the Temple, built of white marble, with golden roof and dome shining against the sky!

How thrilled Jesus was! His heart leapt when He saw His Father's House.

Now there is the last hill to climb. The pilgrims are tired but no one minds. The whole company is full of joy and bursts out into singing.

We can find in our Old Testament some of the lovely words they sang. They are written in the Book of Psalms.

As they looked up at the city they so much loved they sang:

> I will lift up my eyes unto the hills;
> From whence cometh my strength?
> My strength cometh from the Lord.

Then as they gazed upon the beautiful Temple they sang joyfully:

> I was glad when they said unto me
> Let us go into the house of the Lord.

How Jesus would sing those words! That was just what He wanted so much to do—to go into the House of His Heavenly Father.

At last they are at the top of the hill and entering the lovely City through one of its gates. Its streets are swarming with people who have come to the festival; some, from far countries, wearing strange costumes and speaking strange languages which Jesus did not understand.

But He mingled with the crowds and felt happy because, no matter how strange they seemed, they were all children of His Father in Heaven and therefore His own brothers and sisters. He loved them all and longed to tell them this joyful news.

But He did not linger very long about the streets. He was all eagerness to be in the Temple. With what great love and interest He looked upon everything there was to see! The pilgrims stayed for several days at this great festival, and each day Jesus knelt with them and prayed to His Heavenly Father.

Then He found the Rabbis, that is the teachers, in the Temple and sat down before them. He was so eager to learn anything and everything they could teach Him.

The first time boys and girls visited the Temple on becoming twelve years of age, these Rabbis questioned them to see how much they had learned of the Holy Scriptures. And so they began to question Jesus.

But very soon they were filled with astonishment at His knowledge and wisdom. Before very long He was asking them questions so difficult and unusual that they found it very hard to answer them.

I think Jesus must have been disappointed with these masters. He soon found that in some ways He knew more than they did about His Heavenly Father and the kind of things that would please Him.

They must have wondered greatly who this Boy was, where He came from, and who had taught Him.

We know God had taught Him, first through

His good mother, Mary, and afterwards also through His own study of the Bible.

But why did not these Rabbis understand the Bible as Jesus did, though He was only a young boy? It was because they had wrong ideas of God. They would have to quite change their minds and hearts before they would be able to understand God, the loving Father.

Instead, as they grew older they grew proud, then prouder, to be called 'Rabbi'. Years after, when Jesus was a man, wise and wonderful, He would say: 'I am meek and lowly in heart' and 'I do always what pleases My Father.' He was happy to learn as a child; He was happy to be a son, and to serve such a Father.

Well, Jesus was so interested and so happy in His Father's House that when the day came for the return journey home He forgot all about it and did not join his father and mother.

They set out with the company of people from Nazareth and travelled for a whole day before they found out that Jesus was not amongst the other boys and girls. So they had to return to Jerusalem. They were very anxious and troubled about Him and for three days they searched the whole city before they found Him in the Temple.

There He was, still sitting amongst the Rabbis. They stood quietly listening to Him and were as astonished as everyone else at His understanding and answers—and His questions!

Then Jesus saw them and His mother said: 'Child, why have you treated us like this? Your father and I have been so upset about you and have been looking for you everywhere.'

Then Jesus looked at His mother in surprise and said: 'Why did you look everywhere for me, mother? Did you not know that you would be sure to find me here, in my Father's House?'

From that time Mary knew that her Boy's whole thought and life were for His Father in Heaven. Even she, dearly as He loved her, came second.

Jesus must have longed to stay in beautiful Jerusalem and His Father's House. But He went quietly home with Joseph and Mary and was perfectly obedient to them.

He went on living and helping in the little Nazareth home. Day by day he grew bigger and taller as you do, and at the same time He went on learning and becoming wiser. People who knew Him loved Him; and His Heavenly Father constantly smiled upon Him. Jesus was quite sure of that.

AT NAZARETH

In the field of Nazareth,
　Jesus saw the lilies gay,
Lovelier dressed than Solomon
　In his glory, they.
Happy little Jesus said,
　'All these flowers My Father made,
Clothed them, clothed the lovely lily,
　All the flowers—and Me.'

In the lanes of Nazareth
　Walking one day Jesus found
'Neath the trees a little nestling
　Fallen to the ground.
Full of pity, Jesus said,
　'All things that My Father made,
Every one, He loves them dearly,
　Loves this bird—and Me.'

CHAPTER VI

AT NAZARETH

SOME say that at the time Jesus lived in
Nazareth, it was a very wicked place. If that
is right, Jesus must have been very sad to
see the people doing evil. He knew they were
bringing misery and ill-health upon themselves. Wrong-doing always brings its own
punishment sooner or later. Jesus longed to
help these people to do better and to tell
them how sad it made their loving Heavenly
Father to see them injuring themselves.

But certainly Nazareth gave Jesus a great
deal of happiness, for Nazareth was one of the
loveliest places in the world and Jesus loved
everything beautiful.

The little town lay in a wooded hollow up
amongst the hills. Its white houses stood
amongst gardens and vineyards and groves
of olive, fig, orange and pomegranate trees.
In its fields grew innumerable flowers of many
kinds and colours: the lilies Jesus spoke of
were probably brilliant red.

Behind the town a hill rose to about five
hundred feet and from the top Jesus could
see one of the most wonderful of views. He

could see the lovely mountains of Galilee, and Mount Hermon towering above them, always crowned with snow; the lake, called the Sea of Galilee, was dotted with fishing-boats and pleasure-boats, some of the latter belonging to the Roman conquerors and, far away, the sparkling waters of the blue Mediterranean Sea.

Jesus often climbed this hill and gazed in rapture on the lovely scene below.

Then He thought how all this beauty was the handiwork of His Heavenly Father and He joyfully thanked Him for His goodness and love. From this time He formed the habit of climbing this hill when He wanted to talk in quiet to His Father.

An important high road also ran near to Nazareth and Jesus watched caravans of camels continually passing along it, carrying great loads of all kinds of goods from one part of the country to another, or into other countries. In the part of the country where Jesus lived there were people of many nations— the Jews called them Gentiles. And He would see constant processions of them passing along this high road on all kinds of business. He would also see the well-drilled Roman soldiers marching along in their shining armour, the officers looking very fine and grand on their prancing horses.

Jesus was very observant; that is, He looked at everything about Him with keen, open eyes. And, of course, that is one of the best ways to learn. So Jesus learned lessons from all the common things about Him and these He taught later on to men and women, and boys and girls.

Many common things had a hidden meaning to Jesus. The flowers, even the grasses, to Him were living creatures most beautifully dressed by His Father in Heaven. The birds were dear to His Father, fed and cared for by Him. The wind in the trees seemed to Jesus like His Father's voice. The sky was the throne of His Father and the earth was His footstool.

When Jesus saw a flock of sheep they made Him think of a crowd of people needing a shepherd and He wanted to be that Good Shepherd.

Once a terrible storm of wind and rain came and beat furiously about the little town. The houses that were built upon firm, solid ground with good foundations, stood the test of the storm; not one of them fell.

But any house that was built upon soft, shifting sand with no solid foundation, was not able to stand the test of the storm; it fell and it was a very bad fall.

Jesus saw a hidden meaning in all this. He

saw that if we build a strong character by always doing what we know to be right we shall be able to stand if any big temptation, like a big storm, comes to us; we shall not fall.

But if we build a weak character by going the easy way, and not fighting evil in ourselves, then when a big temptation comes we shall fall, and our fall will be very great.

Jesus also saw meanings in the everyday things He saw His mother doing in the home, baking bread, patching clothes, lighting the lamp, looking for lost things. He even saw a meaning when He watched girls and boys playing games in the streets. Later on, in Chapter XI, we shall see how He wove many of these common things into beautiful stories.

But Jesus was getting older now and a change was coming into His life.

You remember how He loved to see His father at work in his carpenter's shop.

One day His father said to Him: 'You will be leaving school soon, sonny. What do you think you would like to do then?'

Jesus looked at some of the beautiful things His father had made, and then answered: 'I should like to make things as you do, father.'

'Then you shall do, my boy,' said His father, patting Him on the back.

'Shall I have a set of tools like yours, I

mean, father?' asked the Boy, looking long-ingly at the chisel, the hammer, and the saw.

'Indeed, you shall,' His father replied, 'and I know you will make very good use of them.'

So Joseph began to teach Jesus the trade of a carpenter. The boy had to learn by making mistakes at first, just as you do, but little by little He became perfect at His job. He liked making ploughs and yokes, and chairs and tables, and lots of other things, and He made them so well that He was always very busy. People soon found they could trust Jesus to put His very best work into everything He did, so He was never short of orders.

Then a sad day came when His good father, Joseph, died. His mother, Mary, was left a poor widow to bring up her young family.

How Jesus worked then, earning all He could to help to keep His mother and His young brothers and sisters! He did all he could to take His father's place in the home.

But although He was so busy, never a day passed that He did not talk to His Heavenly Father and try to find out more and more about Him in the Holy Scriptures.

And more and more He was filled with a great longing to tell everyone about this loving Father.

But He felt it was His duty to stay at home and help the mother He so much loved, until His brothers and sisters were old enough to take care of themselves. And Mary learned to look to her eldest son, Jesus, for help in her many difficulties. He always seemed to find a way through.

So Jesus lived as an ordinary workman until He was thirty years of age. How patient He was!

Then a great change came into His life. Something happened that told Him it was now time to give up the work of a carpenter and to say goodbye to His home and lovely Nazareth. We will now see what He did.

Jesus speaking to the crowd on the shore of Galilee

CHAPTER VII

JESUS MAKES THE GREAT DISCOVERY

ALL the time Jesus was growing up and becoming a man the people were still waiting for the promised Messiah, as they had done for centuries.

You will remember how the Wise Men called Jesus 'The King of the Jews'.

Most of the people hated their Roman conquerors and many of them thought that the Messiah when He came would gather together a great army, throw out the Romans from the land and sit on the throne as their King.

We know they were wrong, but only a few had right ideas about the coming One.

Little did they think their Messiah was living amongst them as a poor and humble workman in a carpenter's shop.

But just about the time when Jesus reached the age of thirty years, there appeared on the banks of the River Jordan a new and wonderful preacher.

He had come from the desert, where he had been living for a number of years, dressed in a cloak of camel's hair and eating only locusts, a kind of large grasshopper, and the honey made by the wild bees that lived in holes in the rocks.

Now this preacher was none other than John, who had once been the little baby God had sent to Elizabeth and her husband in answer to their prayers. You remember the angel had said he would be a great and a good man.

As John grew up it gradually came to him that God had some work He wanted him to do.

So he went into the desert where it was very quiet and lived there all by himself so that he could hear God speak to him.

And God did speak to him, as He did to Samuel (1 Samuel 3), as He does to all who really listen. God spoke in John's heart. He gave him a wonderful message. Then He said that the work He wanted John to do was to give this message to the people.

So John came out from the desert and went to the River Jordan. He stood on the bank of the river and spoke to the people. And this is what he told them: 'The Messiah for whom you have waited so long is close at hand.'

This was the message God had given to John, and when the people heard it their hearts thrilled and they were filled with joy. Soon great crowds of people came to listen to John from all over the country.

But John had something else to say to them which was not so pleasant. Some, perhaps, would not like to hear it.

He said: 'The Messiah has come; He is here amongst you. But you are not ready for Him. You are not good enough to receive Him. He is the Holy One from Heaven.

'Some of you are doing things you know are wrong; quarrelling with one another, taking things that don't belong to you, speaking untruths, being unkind and even cruel. You must change all this and learn to live good lives. Only by so doing can you please the Messiah and God who has sent Him.'

So a few of the people began to understand that their Messiah had not come to cast out and conquer the hated Romans, but to cast out the evil from their hearts. He would not be a king seated upon an earthly throne but be the King of Love. So John was a *herald* announcing the coming of the King, God's Son, and ready to point Him out.

Then they asked John what they must do and John said: 'Some of you are rich and have plenty of good clothes. If you see a poor man in rags because he cannot earn much money, give him some of your clothes. And if you know he is hungry feed him. If you live unselfishly like this you will be pleasing to the Messiah.'

Some soldiers came to John and said: 'What shall we do?'

John told them to be kind instead of cruel, not to frighten people into giving them money, and to be satisfied with the wages they received.

Many people were sorry for their wrong-doing and when they made up their minds to do better, John dipped them in the river.

You have a bath to make your bodies clean, don't you? John dipped these people in the river as a sign that they wanted to have their hearts washed clean from evil. This was called Baptism. So, because John baptized the people, he was called 'John the Baptist'.

Now Jesus, in His workshop, heard of this wonderful new preacher and how great crowds of people were flocking to hear him.

I don't know whether He knew it was His cousin or not.

However that may be, Jesus felt He must go the long journey to hear the new preacher. It meant giving up His carpenter's work, but some of His brothers were now old enough to carry on with it and earn enough money to keep their mother and the family.

So Jesus told them where He was going and why. He asked them to take good care of their mother and their younger brothers and sisters. Then He kissed His mother, said goodbye to them all and set out on His journey.

At last He reached the place on the bank of the River Jordan. There He stood amongst the crowd listening.

But John noticed Him at once, and all the time he was speaking he could not take his eyes from the face of Jesus. He had never seen anyone with a face so pure, so holy, and so good. Yet, at the same time it was a strong face, the face of one who could be very brave and fearless. It made John feel he was a long, long way from being so good himself.

When John had finished speaking, he asked those who intended to lead new lives to come to the water to be baptized.

Quite a large number came. And amongst them was Jesus. But John said to Jesus: '*You* have done nothing wrong to be sorry for. I am not good enough to baptize one like you. I feel *you* should be baptizing *me*.'

But Jesus answered: 'Please do it for me. I want to show all these people that I belong utterly to God and shall spend every moment of My life doing only what pleases Him.'

So Jesus stepped into the river and John baptized him.

Then a wonderful thing happened. Jesus stood in the water looking up to His Heavenly Father and giving Himself joyfully and completely to Him. And as He looked up into the sky He saw the heavens open. And the Spirit of His Father came down and rested upon Him like a beautiful white dove.

Then Jesus heard His Heavenly Father's voice saying: 'You are My own beloved Son; I am well pleased with You.'

Then in a flash Jesus knew who He Himself was. He had made the great discovery! He had had little hints of it before, especially through things His mother, Mary, had told Him. But now He was certain. He was the Messiah, the Christ, the Son of God, and He was filled with very great joy.

John also knew now who Jesus was, for God had said to him: 'When you see the Spirit of God coming down from Heaven like a dove and resting upon Someone you will know that One is the Messiah, the Son of God.'

So now Jesus knew that before He was born in Bethlehem He had lived with His Father in Heaven. He knew that His Father, who loved Him so much, had given Him to the world. He had sent Him into this world because He loved every man, woman, girl and boy so much. And He knew His Father had sent Him just to tell this good news.

He knew now what His Heavenly Father wanted Him to do. And it was the very thing He had so longed to do ever since He was a boy. It was what He had told His mother He wanted to do more than anything else in the world. How wonderful it all was!

'Oh,' He cried, 'I don't mind what happens to me or where I go if only I can do this wonderful work given me by my Father! I shall spend every moment of my life doing that work and never rest until it is finished. It will be all my happiness.'

Then Jesus felt, as John the Baptist had felt, that He must get away from the crowds and go to some very quiet place where He could be alone with His Father. He wanted to talk to Him and listen to His voice telling Him how He wanted Him to do this great work.

But Jesus, like you and me, heard *other voices*, some good, some bad.

Adam and Eve heard the Voice of God in the garden. When they followed that, all was well. But sometimes another voice was heard, sounding quite pleasant and harmless.

We all know the voice of hunger, but if you were doing your best at an examination and a clock struck dinner-time, you'd shut your ears to that voice, wouldn't you? But how long would you, or could you, keep that up?

There's the voice of Self—'let me have that', 'let me do that', 'let me show you, I know how'—with a little emphasis on the 'I'! That voice sometimes gets louder, doesn't it?—'I know better than you', 'Let me have *my* way'.

Now that voice may drown *The Voice*.

Though Jesus knew, or just because He knew He was the Messiah, He said: 'It's a son's work I have to do; I shall best do it if I keep in mind that it's His work first; I must see to it that I do His Will. I must listen to the Voice, and sometimes wait for the Voice, telling me how He wants me to do His great work.'

When there's a hubbub of talk in your house, you can't hear clearly the voice on the wireless can you? You want quiet first.

The Voice called Jesus to the wilderness, with bare rock and sand around, and blue sky above, to live alone, alone with the Father.

And Jesus joyfully obeyed, determined to learn how to 'play the game'. He had done that for Mary and Joseph and His family— now for the Heavenly Father. What will Jesus do?

Jesus told His disciples about it later on and we have it in the Gospels, especially 'Matthew', 'Mark', and 'Luke', in visions, or pictures if you like, in the mind—three pictures showing:

THE GREAT DISCOVERY TESTED
AND FOUND TRUE.

In the midst of loneliness, wild wastes

around, and wild beasts too. Yes. But around Him just as surely Jesus felt, without seeing, the everlasting arms of the Father, always with Him, always loving Him; also disciplining Him, exposing Him to severe temptation, to strengthen His love and loyalty.

Jesus has to learn to live a man's life, to suffer hunger and weariness, to live with us, the poorest and weakest and worst of us, to live for us, a brave friend. He knows the secret of that is to live for God the Father.

He must be a prophet, pointing men to God the Father; a pioneer, fearless for God; a shepherd of souls, knowing every need of people old and young, guiding, enfolding, guarding them, and ready at their need and at the call of *The Voice* to give His life for them.

The Great Discovery helped Jesus to accept the Great Commandment (Deuteronomy 6^{45}) and to learn the second, like it (Matthew 22$^{34-40}$) and to teach, by stories and His own life, the New Commandment (John 13^{34}).

He gave His disciples, and us, these three pictures to show how careful He was to find out, as He prayed, how to test and keep in His work the laws by which He saw His Father worked, and how delightful it was to Him to fulfil His Father's will, and to give

to others out of the love the Father so freely
gave Him.

1. A grand Christian, who had once been
in 'the far country', but had come back to the
great love of the Father, said: 'Love and do
what you like.' You yourself will learn to put
the word 'God' before 'and'. A lovely hymn
teaches us to ask 'that I may love what Thou
dost love and do what Thou wouldst do'.

Jesus had to be on guard when a voice said,
as if wanting to help, 'You can do as you like
—you, the Son of God. You are hungry, but
you can change these stones about you into
bread. Do it, then you can stay on here,
talking with God as long as you like. And
You know those words in Your Bible: "He
gave them manna to eat." '

But Jesus knew His Bible better than that
and went on quoting the passage (Deuteronomy 8³): '. . . man lives not only by food,
but by every word that comes out of the
mouth of God.'

And God's words, and especially 'You are
My beloved Son, I am well pleased with You,'
still ringing in His ears, like the music of a
trumpet, gave Him joy and courage and
strength to go on.

And the Father gave more and more of His
Spirit as Jesus went on.

As Jesus said, He would never do anything

except He saw His Father doing it. He had seen His Father growing lots and lots of corn to make bread, but He took time for that, time for turning stones into the soil that corn feeds on so slowly but surely—and His time is best.

2. You see, Jesus had *one ambition*. God was 'all his Happiness'. Now that kept Him from wrong ambition.

Jesus had pride in His Father (John 14[31]); He had pride in His job, just as when He was in the carpenter's shop; but it was pure, unselfish pride.

I wonder if you've asked yourself: 'I'm proud of my prizes—is that right?' Jesus could be hungry; we know He was. He needed sleep, like us. He felt weak often; but His strength lay in His love, and love meets pride without fear, and can take self out of pride, and turn self towards God in a great desire to be worthy of His favour, and *not to 'trespass'* on it.

When He puts us 'on parole', on our honour, we must honour His orders or we shall dishonour Him.

God gave to His Son power to work miracles, which seemed at first all for good, but he came to see that the crowds might be impressed, but wrongly impressed, by some miracles, and especially when they said: 'How clever!' Then Jesus began to see they were looking for 'signs in the sky' and not for free gifts from God which turn men's hearts toward Him.

God showed Him in a vision that if, for example, from a high point on the temple, He threw Himself down into the crowd, He would be breaking the command, 'Thou shalt not tempt the Lord thy God,' and going against His own Prayer, 'Hallowed be Thy Name,' and also against His Father's will, who wants us to be brave but not foolish.

For it would have been just as foolish as though you took no care in crossing the road and then said God should not have allowed a car to hurt you. Or as foolish as though you ate things you knew were bad for you, or let yourself get wet through over and over again and then expected your Heavenly Father to keep you from being ill.

When we do such things we break God's laws, and we cannot blame Him if we have to suffer. So Jesus was on guard against the reckless risking even of His own life. Even that belonged to God, and the day would come when the Father would claim it from His Son to save the world.

3. And that links up with a third word or vision that came to Jesus during those forty days in the wilderness.

He had been helped twice to say '*No*' by knowing God's word in the Book and by loving Him. He felt His Father was trusting Him to choose right rules for His work; the Father was indeed disciplining His Son.

You have felt sometimes, when God has strengthened you to meet stern temptations, a great reverence filling your heart and a great *desire to worship* Him as your King; and, like Isaiah, with a big '*Yes*' to last life-long, to say, 'Here am I, send me' (Isaiah 6).

Jesus learned to put aside love of praise from men, calls to 'take care of yourself' and 'safety first', short cuts to success, 'winning the world before I die', entreaties to avoid a shameful death on the Cross. Peter cried out: 'God forbid that,' but Jesus answered: 'Get behind me, Tempter, you're in the way, stopping me in the way pointed out by the loving Father.'

The motto of a great missionary was: 'The utmost for the highest.' And so, with Jesus, worship of anything less than the highest gave way to this: 'Thou shalt worship the Lord, thy God, and Him only shalt thou serve.'

Right to the end of His life He was tempted just as we are, but never in the very least did He yield. Never once did He do wrong. But He knows how hard it is for us to fight temptation because He had such stern fights Himself. And if we ask Him He will always help us to conquer.

CHAPTER VIII

HOW JESUS MADE FRIENDS

JESUS did not return to His home in Nazareth after this. That was not because He loved His mother and His brothers and sisters any less, but because His Heavenly Father told Him it was now time to begin His great work. This was to tell the Good News of the Father's wonderful love to as many people as He could everywhere.

Jesus began by the side of the lake He had so often seen when a boy, the Sea of Galilee. It was a large sheet of water about thirteen miles long and six miles across. Round the shores of this lake was just the place for Jesus because there were so many people to listen to Him.

The country of Galilee in which the lake lay was very fertile, that is, everything grew very well there. So a great many people earned their living by working on the land. Some were farmers and grew corn. Mountains sloping down gently to the lake, grew splendid crops on their sides.

At their feet were groves of fruit trees and all over the country vines grew with their clusters of fine grapes. All these needed workers to tend them.

Also the lake was teeming with fish and this brought many fishermen and their families to live there.

So both inland and all round the lake were several towns and villages where all these people lived.

Scores of fishing-boats were always passing to and fro on the lake, along with the pleasure-boats and passenger-boats for taking people from one side of the lake to the other. It must have been a pretty sight, especially as the pleasure-boats of the Roman lords were very gay.

So you see what a splendid part of the country this was for the work Jesus wanted to do. There were always crowds of people about for Him to talk to.

So here He began to tell the joyful news of the Father in Heaven; of His great and never-ceasing love for everyone. He told many beautiful stories and spoke so wonderfully that the people said: 'We have never heard anyone speak like this before.' Soon big crowds began to follow Him about from place to place, afraid to miss any of His beautiful words.

Jesus soon began to make friends. Some of these became His special friends and companions, going about with Him from town to town and village to village. Several of these friends were fishermen.

He was standing by the side of the lake talking about the love of the Father, but there was such a big crowd pressing upon Him that He was almost being pushed into the water. Just then He saw two fishing-boats drawn up on the beach by the edge of the lake. The fishermen had gone out of them and were busy washing their nets in the water.

Jesus thought that if one of those boats could be pushed a little out into the water He could get into it and speak to the people from it and so be both seen and heard much better.

One of the boats belonged to a fisherman called Simon. Now Jesus had seen Simon before. He was an old friend of John the Baptist.

One day after John had baptized Jesus and had found out who He was, he was standing with two of his friends when Jesus came walking by.

John pointed to Jesus and said: 'Look! that is the Lamb of God; you must leave me and be His friends now.' This was very unselfish and noble of John, because he loved his friends. But he knew God had sent him to point people to Jesus, His Son. So he was willing to lose his friends for the sake of Jesus.

The good Samaritan

So John's two friends followed Jesus, hoping they might get to know Him.

Soon Jesus turned round and, seeing them following Him, said: 'What are you looking for?'

They said to Him: 'Master, where do You live?'

Jesus replied: 'Come, and you will see.'

So, feeling very pleased, they walked along with Jesus to the house where He was staying just then and went in with Him. It was about four o'clock in the afternoon and they stayed with Jesus the rest of the day.

He told them about His great work and said He would be very glad if they would help Him. They were delighted and had a very happy time.

One of these two friends was called Andrew. Afterwards he went in great excitement to find his brother who was Simon. He said to him: 'You must come along at once. We have had a wonderful time! We have found the Messiah.'

Simon immediately stopped washing his fishing nets and ran along with his brother to see Jesus.

When Jesus saw him, He said: 'I know who *you* are! You are Simon. I shall call you by another name also. You shall be called Peter, which means a rock.' So ever after Simon was called Simon Peter or just Peter.

E

Jesus then said: 'Will you push your boat a little out into the water, Peter?' Simon Peter was only too glad to do this for Jesus. Then Jesus got into the boat and, sitting down in it, talked to the people.

When Jesus had finished speaking, He said to Peter: 'Push your boat out further into deep water and let down your nets for a catch.'

But Peter answered: 'Oh Master, we have been out fishing all night and have let down our nets over and over again but we have caught not a single fish. But all the same, as you have told us to do it, we will try again.'

So he and his brother Andrew let down the nets and at once they caught a great multitude of fish. And the nets were so full that they began to break!

Then they called to their partners, James and John, in the other boat, to come and help them. So they came and they filled both the boats so that they began to sink with the great weight of fish.

Then Peter saw there was something very wonderful about Jesus and he was afraid because he felt he was not good enough to be with Him.

And he cried out: 'Oh Master, depart from me; I am a sinful man,' and he fell down at Jesus' knees.

But Jesus said to him: 'Fear not! From

this time you shall be a fisher of men.' Jesus meant that He would teach Peter how to lead men to God.

James and John were also filled with wonder when they saw the amazing catch of fishes.

Then they brought the boats to land. But they had all decided to be friends and helpers of Jesus. So they left their boats and nets and everything they had, and followed Him.

Now Jesus knew they had a friend called Philip, so He said: 'We must have Philip also.' So Jesus went Himself and found Philip and he also became a friend of Jesus.

Philip was so happy that he felt he must bring someone else to Jesus and off he went to find his friend Nathanael.

Philip found him in his garden, in a very quiet corner under a fig tree. Nathanael had gone there to pray to God in secret where no one could see him. He was a really good man so God always listened to his prayers.

Nathanael was very different from some religious men who at that time used to stand in the streets where they could be best seen and say long prayers so that people would think them very good. Jesus spoke very sternly to some of these men because they only thought about their own glory and often did evil in secret. We call this sort of people hypocrites; they are just pretenders.

Well, if you want to 'find out' Nathanael for yourself, look him up in John 1$^{43\text{-}51}$.

Jesus made friends with all kinds of people. It did not matter to Him whether they were rich or poor or whether they were thought well of by other people or not. So long as people were sincere, which means that they didn't pretend to be better than they really were, Jesus would make friends with them.

The Pharisees thought themselves to be religious, but many of them just pretended, and were very angry with Jesus for making friends of people they themselves called 'publicans—that is, collectors of taxes for their Roman masters. The Pharisees hated these and expected to be delivered from them by the coming Messiah.

You'll find stories of these hated tax-collectors in Luke 19$^{1\text{-}10}$ and Luke 5$^{27\text{-}32}$.

Four of His friends wrote books about Him. Matthew wrote a very beautiful one, telling us many of the wonderful words and stories of Jesus.

John also wrote a lovely book about Jesus. Some people like John's book best of all.

Another book was written by a friend of Peter, called Mark. Peter told him all the beautiful things Jesus said and did, everything he could remember, and Mark wrote them in his book.

Then, after Jesus had gone back to His Father in Heaven, one of those who learned to love Him, whose name was Luke, also wrote a very interesting book about Him. He was a doctor, very interested in sick folk and 'lost' folk and how Jesus helped them. He was very helpful to Paul the missionary.

So that makes four books about Jesus and, as you know, they are called the four Gospels. The word Gospel simply means Good News. So each of these books tells us the Good News Jesus brought about our Heavenly Father who loves us so dearly and who forgives us everything we do wrong the moment we are sorry and try to be better.

Altogether Jesus chose twelve men to be his special friends and helpers. But, of course, they had to learn a great deal before they could help Jesus really well. So He began to teach them. That is why these twelve men are called the twelve disciples. A disciple means a learner. Any of us can be a disciple of Jesus if we let Him teach us and try to do as He tells us.

The twelve went about with Jesus from place to place, watching everything He did and listening to all that He said.

We see how Jesus made friends. One friend you remember saw that Jesus was the Lamb of God, who would give His life for others.

This friend was himself ready to give his life for the King.

Now perhaps you would like to hear a little more of John the Baptist and what became of him.

You remember how he was born in answer to the prayers of his father and mother, and how the angel said he would be a good and a great man.

You know how the words of the angel came true. God spoke to him in the desert and gave him the wonderful message that the Messiah, God's Son, had come.

Then John gave this message to the people and told them how to prepare to receive the Messiah by leading good lives; and he baptized those who were sorry for their evil ways and wanted their hearts to be washed clean.

Then Jesus came to be baptized and John found out He was the Messiah when the Spirit of God, like a white dove, came down from Heaven and rested upon him.

Then you remember how noble and unselfish John was in giving up his own dear friends and disciples to Jesus. And when anyone came to John, hoping to hear him speak again, he would send them to Jesus telling them they must listen to Him now. He said: 'Jesus will grow greater and greater but I shall now be less and less important.'

Perhaps John thought his work was now finished and he could go quietly home. But no. God still had some work for him to do and very hard work, too. It was something that only a true and a brave man could do. But John was a very brave man.

God said to him: 'Go to the palace of King Herod and tell him that he is doing a very evil thing.'

That was a very dangerous thing for John to do. Herod would certainly be very angry at the messenger with such a message.

Kings thought nothing in those days of killing people they were angry with. But John went and paid for his bravery with his life. We may well call him the first Christian martyr. And a martyr, who gives his life, as John did, for God, is also a witness whose life and death 'speak' for God and His Kingdom.

And as Jesus said: 'There has not been born into this world anyone greater than John the Baptist.'

Chapter IX

JESUS THE GREAT HEALER

1. VERY beautiful and wonderful things the twelve disciples saw and heard as they went about with Jesus.

The heart of Jesus was made of love. No one who ever lived on this earth loved as Jesus loved. He loved like God, the Heavenly Father, and God *is* love.

Everything Jesus did, he did because He loved. That is why He never did wrong. Jesus said if we let love tell us what to do and are always ruled by love, we also shall do right and please God.

Love gave Jesus a wonderful gift and that was the power to heal. He was full of pity for all sick and suffering people and He longed to make them well and happy again. It made the heart of Jesus ache to see anyone suffering.

There was only one thing the sick or unhappy people had to do. That was to believe Jesus could and would make them better. Believing He could do it and was willing was called 'having faith' in Jesus. He often said to people he had cured: 'It was your faith that healed you.'

For instance—there was a poor woman who had been very ill for twelve years and had spent almost all her money on doctors' bills. Yet she was no better, but rather grew worse.

She had heard of Jesus and one day she saw Him. His face was so loving and kind that she said to herself: 'If I can only so much as touch His clothes, I feel sure I shall be healed.'

She was a shy woman and too timid to speak to Jesus or stand before Him. But what great faith she had!

Jesus was surrounded by a great crowd of people, but she fought her way through, weak as she was, until she was just behind Him. Then she stretched out her hand and just touched the fringe of His long robe. Instantly she felt new life flow through her and knew she was cured.

But she was afraid. She thought Jesus might be angry with her if He knew what she had done. So she tried to steal quietly away without saying anything about it.

But Jesus stopped and called out: 'Who touched Me?' The crowd stood still and Jesus looked at the people nearest to Him, but they all denied touching Him.

Then Peter said: 'Master, there is such a big crowd all about you that some must have pressed against you.'

But Jesus knew this was different. He knew someone had touched Him because they needed Him. So He said: 'Someone did touch Me; I felt healing power flow out from Me.'

Then the woman saw it was no use trying to hide herself from Jesus, so she came before Him trembling. Falling upon her knees at His feet she told Him before all the crowd why she had touched Him and how she was instantly cured.

Then Jesus said to her: 'My dear child, it was your faith that cured you. Do not be afraid. Go home and be happy.'

2. Sometimes people suffering from a very terrible disease came to Jesus. This was called leprosy and no doctor could cure it. Not then; now doctors can.

It gradually ate away the flesh of the poor sick person and he was covered with dreadful sores. After much suffering he died.

Other people could very easily catch the disease from him, so he had to leave his home, his family and his friends and go right away to live with other lepers in a leper-colony or camp. His friends brought him food and drink. But they dare not go near him because of the infection. So they placed the food on the ground some distance from the leper-colony and went away. Then he came out and got it.

If he walked along a road he had to warn people to keep away from him by calling out 'Unclean, unclean'. Then people knew he was a leper. So you see the poor lepers were very miserable and lonely people.

Well, one of these lepers heard about the pity and love of Jesus and of the wonderful power God had given Him to heal the sick.

It was not easy for this man to believe Jesus could cure a disease like leprosy that was known to be incurable.

But every day he heard of the wonderful things Jesus was doing and hope began to grow in his heart.

Every day he went along the road looking out for Jesus. He shouted to so many people passing along: 'Do you know where Jesus is?' that at last it became known what this poor ragged man was waiting for.

At last someone called out to him: 'Here is Jesus coming along the road.' He knew it was Jesus although he had never seen Him before. He knew by those kind eyes looking so lovingly upon him.

So he fell upon his face on the ground and cried out: 'O Lord, if only you will, I know you can make me clean and healthy again.'

Then Jesus did something that no one else would have dared to do. The disciples must have been very surprised and shocked to see Him do it.

Jesus crossed the road to the leper, came quite close to him with no fear of taking the dreadful disease, and stretching out His hand He touched the leper. That was the first time the leper had been touched since he had become a leper.

He had said to Jesus: 'If you are only willing you can cure me.' And Jesus answered: 'I am willing; be clean and healthy again.'

At once the awful disease left the man and his flesh became as sweet and clean as a little child's. And that was because this leper had faith in Jesus.

3. On another day two blind men heard that Jesus was passing by and they followed Him down the road crying out: 'Have mercy on us, have mercy on us, dear Christ.'

Then someone told them that Jesus had gone into a friend's house. But they did not give up. They followed Him inside and begged Him to give them their sight.

Jesus said to them: 'Do you believe I am able to do this?' They answered: 'Yes, Lord, we do.'

Then He touched their eyes and said: 'As you have had faith in Me it shall be done to you.' And their eyes were opened.

4. Sometimes sick people were healed

because their friends helped. If you would like to read how an army captain, a centurion of the hated Roman army, won the love of even Jews, how they came to Jesus pleading for him, because his servant (a missionary in Ceylon would call him 'boy') was near death, and the captain would do anything to save him, then read Luke 7^{1-10}. And another story: how friends of a man paralysed and bedridden, carried the man, bed and all, and let the lot with loving skill through the roof, so that the man might be healed by Jesus, you will find in Luke 5^{17-26}.

Chapter X

JESUS AND HIS DISCIPLES

ALL this time the disciples had been watching these things as they went from place to place with Jesus. There seemed to be nothing He could not do if only people had faith in Him. And Jesus told them they must trust their Heavenly Father in just the same way.

After they had given up their work and left everything to be friends and helpers of Jesus, they were very poor and sometimes didn't even know where their next meal was to come from.

Often the people Jesus had healed, or those who had listened to His beautiful stories, would show their love and thankfulness by taking Him and some of His disciples into their homes. Then they would have food and beds to sleep in for a time.

But when no one took them in and they were far from their own homes, and almost without money, the disciples sometimes got anxious and troubled and said to each other: 'How shall we get something to eat and drink?'

Then Jesus said to them: 'Where is your faith in your Heavenly Father? Look at the birds, they neither sow nor reap to get their food, nor do they store food in barns. Yet your Heavenly Father feeds them. Don't you think you are worth much more to Him than birds?'

Then when the disciples' clothes began to look shabby they said to one another: 'How shall we get new clothes when these are worn out?'

But Jesus said to them: 'You would not ask these questions if you really trusted your Heavenly Father! Look at the lovely lilies growing in the field. They neither spin nor weave clothes for themselves. Your Heavenly Father clothes them and they are far more beautifully dressed even than King Solomon in all his gorgeous robes.

And if God so clothes the wild flowers that, after all, only live a few days and then are thrown into the oven to dry for kindling fires, will He not much more clothe you, His dear children? What little faith you have!

So don't worry yourselves saying: "What shall we eat?" or "What shall we drink?" or "How shall we get clothes?" It is only those who have no love for their Heavenly Father who are always troubling themselves about these things. If you love Him best of all, and spend your life in serving Him and trying to please Him, He will see that you have all you need. You have enough for today; don't be anxious about tomorrow. You will find it will be all right when tomorrow comes. Don't meet trouble half-way.

Some of you are fathers. Suppose one of your boys came to you for a slice of bread, would you give him a stone? Or if he asked you for some fish would you give him a snake? Of course you would not! What sort of a father would you be?

Then if you fathers who are far from perfect, give good gifts to your children, how much more will your Heavenly Father, who is perfectly good and loving, give good things to you, His dear children, when you ask Him for them!'

One day Jesus wanted to be alone with His disciples in order to give both them and Himself a rest from the ceaseless crowds of people, for sometimes they had not had time even to eat.

The disciples also were tired because they had only just returned from a tour on which they had been sent by Jesus (Luke 10^{1-24}) and needed to rest at once. So He said: 'Come, we will go to some quiet place by ourselves and rest awhile.'

Then he took them to a place at the far end of the lake away from all towns and villages.

But the people soon found out where Jesus

The two disciples, doing the bidding of Jesus, come seeking a colt

had gone and followed Him, some by boat and a great many on foot, walking a long way round the lake.

Like a shepherd Jesus cared for the sick people in the crowd and cured them of their diseases, and He comforted the sad and lonely ones.

Then He talked to them about the love of their Heavenly Father and told them such beautiful stories that they never tired of listening to Him. They stayed with Him for three days and ate up all the food they had brought with them.

When the evening of the third day came, the disciples came to Jesus and said: 'These people must be very hungry; they are far away from shops and houses where they might get something to eat. Send them away to the villages where they can buy food.'

But Jesus said: 'If they walk all that way they will faint by the roadside with hunger and weariness. There is no need for them to go away; you give them something to eat.'

Now Jesus knew the disciples had no food with them to feed this great multitude of people (there were about five thousand men besides the women and children).

But He was testing them to see if their faith in Him was growing. Also Jesus expected them to know that He would never tell them

F

to do something impossible, or something He would not help them to do.

But they looked at Him in surprise and said: 'Why, even if we spent two hundred pence on bread it would not be nearly enough.' Two hundred pence was really more than five pounds.

Then Jesus asked them: 'How many loaves have you?'

Andrew said : 'There is a lad here who has five loaves and two fishes, but what good are they amongst all these people?'

'Bring them here to Me,' Jesus said.

So Andrew brought the boy with his basket of loaves and fishes to Jesus. And, of course, he was only too pleased to let Jesus have it.

Then Jesus said to the disciples: 'Make the people all sit down in groups.'

So they arranged the people in ranks of hundreds and of fifties and they sat down on the green grass.

Then Jesus took the boy's five loaves and two fishes in His hands and looking up to Heaven He said a blessing over them.

Then He broke the loaves and divided the fishes and gave them to the disciples. And they walked down the grass lanes between the companies of peoples and set the food before them.

And however many times the disciples came back to Jesus for more food for the people His hands were never empty. And all that great multitude had as much as they could eat and were satisfied.

Then Jesus said: 'Gather up the fragments so that nothing is wasted.'

So the disciples took round baskets and filled twelve of them with pieces of bread and fish left over.

Then everyone saw what a wonderful thing Jesus had done. And they said one to another: 'Surely this is the Messiah whom God promised to send into the world.'

Then they came swarming round Jesus crying: 'Come and be our King! Come and be our King!'

They wanted Jesus to make them into an army to fight for Him and to put Him on a throne.

But, as we know, Jesus didn't want to be a king of that kind. He only wanted to be king in their hearts and lives, to make them pure and good.

So He sent all the people away quietly to their homes and then He climbed a hill and prayed there all by Himself to his loving Heavenly Father.

One day a number of mothers brought their little babies to Jesus that He might pray for them and bless them.

The disciples thought Jesus would not want

to be bothered with babies, so they tried to drive the mothers away.

But they were thinking quite wrongly, once again, about Jesus. He loved the little babies and told the disciples they were unkind to drive them away. He said: 'Let the little children come to Me and do not stop them. The Kingdom of Heaven is full of little children.'

Then He took the babies in His arms, laid His kind hands upon their heads and blessed them.

> When mothers of Salem
> Their children brought to Jesus,
> The stern disciples drove them back
> And bade them to depart;
> But Jesus saw them ere they fled,
> And sweetly smiled, and kindly said:
> Suffer the children to come unto Me.
>
> For I will receive them,
> And fold them in My bosom;
> I'll be a shepherd to these Lambs,
> O drive them not away!
> For if their hearts to Me they give,
> They shall with Me in glory live:
> Suffer the children to come unto Me.

Another time the disciples were walking along a road with Jesus when they dropped behind and began arguing and almost quarrelling about something. They went on like this until they came to the house where they were staying just then; perhaps it was Peter's house.

When they were all settled down in the room, Jesus looked at them and said: 'What were you arguing about as we walked along the road?'

But the disciples were ashamed to tell Jesus, because they had been almost quarrelling about which of them would be the greatest in the Kingdom of Heaven.

Jesus knew all about it and called the twelve to Him and they stood around Him.

Then He took a little child, perhaps it was Peter's little boy, and stood him in the middle of them.

Then He lifted the little one on to His knee and said: 'Unless you change in your hearts and become like little children you cannot even enter into the Kingdom of Heaven. The greatest in God's Kingdom are those who are humble like this little child, not struggling to be first but willing to be last and the servant of all. You must copy My example. I did not come in order to have servants waiting upon Me like the great ones of this world. I came to be a servant Myself and even to give My life for everyone.'

Later on Jesus showed His disciples how true this was. Jesus called Himself a servant. Now one of the duties of a servant in that country was to have a bowl of water and a towel ready to wash the dusty feet of his master or his master's friends when they entered the house.

One evening Jesus and His disciples went to a house to have supper together. Now Jesus was their Master, so when they came in from the dusty roads outside they ought to have got water and a towel and washed His feet.

But none of them did so. Not one of them was kind enough to do this for the Master who was so kind to them. And much less did it enter the heads of any of them to do this for one another. But Jesus made them feel very much ashamed of themselves.

While supper was still going on He rose from the table and taking off His outer garments He laid them on one side.

Then He tied a towel round His waist just as the servants would have done and poured water into a bowl.

Then bending down before each disciple in turn He washed their feet and wiped them with the towel He had round Him exactly as though He were their servant.

Peter was terribly ashamed and said: 'I will never let you wash my feet!'

But Jesus said: 'Unless I wash you, Peter, you cannot belong to Me.' Then Peter wanted

Jesus to wash him *all over* because he wanted so much to belong to Jesus.

When Jesus had washed all their feet, He put His outer garments on again and sat down.

Then He said to them: 'Do you understand why I have done this to you? You call Me your Master and Lord and that is right, for so I am. If I, then, your Lord and Master, have washed your feet, you ought also to wash one another's feet. I have given you an example that you should do as I have done.'

But perhaps some of you girls and boys will say: 'We can't do this because it is not the custom in this country.'

That is true. But Jesus only meant it to be an example of the sort of thing we must be willing to do for one another when needful. He meant that we should never think anything too mean or lowly to do for one another. We must not think ourselves above anyone else.

There was a time when it was considered to be a disgrace for a girl to be a nurse because she would have to wash and dress little ones or sick ones and do even more lowly duties for all classes of people. 'No lady,' they said, 'would be a nurse.'

It was Florence Nightingale who, by her Christ-like example, first showed how wrong this idea was. She went across the sea and nursed poor wounded soldiers, doing anything and everything for them. Like Jesus, she showed what a noble thing it is to serve other people and forget ourselves.

Some people came to Jesus and told Him they wanted to be His disciples, who didn't understand what that meant. They thought it would be nothing but happiness and excitement—having a good time.

But Jesus said they must sit down quietly and think about it first, because it was a disgrace to take on such a thing and then give it up again.

'You cannot be My disciples,' He said, 'unless you are willing to give up everything you have.'

One day a young man came to Jesus and said: 'Master, I will follow you wherever you may go.'

But Jesus knew he hadn't thought about it, so He said to him: 'Birds have their nests and foxes have their holes to live and sleep in, but I, the Messiah, have no place to lay My head.' Jesus meant to say to this young man: 'Are you willing to live as I do; to give up friends and home, if necessary, to follow Me?' That is what many missionaries have done and are still doing, because they have obeyed the call of Jesus to go over the seas to tell the Good News.

Another day a very rich young man came

to Jesus and said: 'Good Master, what shall I do to inherit eternal life?'

That meant: 'What shall I do in order that I may live forever with God in Heaven when I leave this world?'

Jesus replied: 'You know the Commandments do you not?'

'Yes,' the young man answered, 'I have kept all the Commandments since I was a boy until now.'

That was very good, was it not? But Jesus knew it wasn't enough for that young man. Jesus knew he loved his riches and his treasures more than his Heavenly Father or the Heavenly Home.

So Jesus said to him: 'There is one thing you still have to do. Sell all you have and give the money you get to the poor, and you shall have treasure in Heaven. Then come and follow Me.'

When the young man heard these words of Jesus he became very sorrowful. Then he turned and walked away for he could not bring himself to give up his riches; he loved them far too much.

Then Jesus said: 'How hard it is for those who have riches to enter into the Kingdom of God. It is easier for a camel to go through a needle's eye than for a rich man to enter into the Kingdom of God.'

But Jesus also said: 'The things which are impossible with men are possible with God.' So if God ever asks us in our hearts to give up something that is very dear to us, He will give us the strength to do it. If we really love our Heavenly Father before everything else, it will be easy to give up things for His sake.

Jesus often told His disciples they would have great joy in their hearts if they followed Him faithfully and helped Him to tell the Good News. But they would often be made to suffer. He told them that wicked men would often be as cruel to them as fierce wolves are to the sheep. They would be caught and taken before rulers and kings. They would be whipped and thrown into prison and any time they might be killed, and all because they were friends and helpers of Jesus.

Then He said: 'Don't expect to be treated better than your Master. If they say evil things about Me they will also say them about you. If they persecute Me they will persecute you.

But never be afraid of those who are only able to kill your body, but are not able to kill your soul, which is the real *you* that will live forever in the Heavenly Home.

But be very much afraid of those who try to make you do wrong and so separate you from your Heavenly Father. That is the worst thing that can happen to you. You would be children of Satan.

But if you are children of your Heavenly Father, everything will be all right whatever happens to you. You are so dear to Him that He loves every hair of your head.

Sparrows are very common little birds. You know you can buy two of them for a farthing. Yet your Father knows if one of them falls to the ground. Then what about you? Don't you think you are far more valuable to Him than many sparrows?'

If you read that book in the New Testament called 'The Acts of the Apostles' you will see that the disciples, who were then called 'apostles' had to suffer, just as Jesus had told them they would. And you will see how they suffered joyfully because it was for Jesus. They were full of joy because they were allowed to carry on His work.

People still have to suffer because they are friends and helpers of Jesus. But because they love Him they suffer joyfully and are proud to be called His disciples.

You will remember that when Jesus was a boy He watched everything His mother did in that little home of Nazareth.

He watched her light the lamp. And she didn't put it on a table as is often done in this country, but on a lamp-stand, a tall pedestal. This made the light shine all over the room for everyone there.

Now Jesus told His disciples their lives must be like that light for everyone to see. They must shine in the world. Then it would be as plain to see they were His disciples as it was to see those villages, and Jesus pointed to the many villages built on the sides or slopes of the hills.

'You are the light of the world,' He said, and 'a city set on a hill cannot be hid.'

Another thing Jesus had seen His mother do was this. She sometimes had a piece of meat that she wanted to keep good for a few days. What did she do? She sprinkled it all over with salt. This kept it from going bad.

Jesus said to the disciples: 'Your lives must be like that salt. They must help to make and keep the world sweet and good.'

He said: 'You are the salt of the earth.'

So He said: 'You must always have a picture of your Heavenly Father before you. He is perfect. You must never be satisfied until you also are perfect.'

Later on the disciples became what Jesus wanted them to be. They became a light in the world that has never been put out. That light is still shining. It is the Light Jesus gave, who said: 'I am the Light of the world.'

CHAPTER XI

JESUS THE WONDERFUL
STORY-TELLER

You will remember how observant Jesus was as a boy and how He learned from the most ordinary things about Him.

That is what scientists do today, isn't it? Have you thought of Jesus as a scientist?

One of His very shortest stories (Mark 4^{26-29}) is like a scientist talking with a farmer, about one of the deep secrets of Nature, how the seed and the soil are suited to each other. On your holidays, on the golden sand you gather lovely round stones and coloured shells and make a pretty pattern pressing them into the sand, and then what?

But when you gently push a tiny seed (very beautiful to look at through the 'lookers' as a little boy I knew called the microscope) into soil, then *you* need hardly do anything else; but *Someone* sets something, alive inside, growing, living in the soil, sending a root into the soil and getting something out of it: and so harvest comes.

And so comes the Kingdom of Heaven, the Kingdom of God where people love and serve

God, 'Our Father', and where all people pray 'Our Father . . . *Thy* Kingdom come: *Thy* will be done.'

Often, when a boy, He had gazed with pleasure on the golden cornfields waving on the gentle hillsides by the Sea of Galilee, coming down almost to the water's edge.

He had noticed the footpath running down the middle of the field, trodden hard by men's feet and horses' feet. He had seen here and there the rocks of the hillside jutting up through the corn, and large thorn bushes flourishing in some places. Jesus could see a meaning in all this and he wove it all into a story. It was called:

(1) THE STORY OF THE SOWER. Or 'Different Kinds of Soil.' (Matthew 13.)

Jesus also told two stories to show how God's Kingdom grows:

(2) THE STORY OF 'THE MUSTARD SEED.' Or 'How the Kingdom of Heaven grows on earth, almost unnoticed, from a very small beginning'; and

(3) THE STORY OF THE LEAVEN.

Just as Jesus's mother on baking day would put some leaven, or yeast, or barm, into the flour and so make it 'rise', with bubbles you can watch rising, and you know this will make it, when baked, sweet in the mouth and easy to digest—so this Kingdom grows, and spreads 'like fire' as we say, not like wild fire, but like a kindly flame, from one to another:

'So let the love of Jesus come,
And set thy soul ablaze.'

Then others will 'catch the flame'.

So the Kingdom of Heaven, the rule of love, spreads and grows from one to another.

When anyone really knows how glorious the Kingdom of God is, they will give anything to belong to it. Jesus told two stories to explain this. The first one is called:

(4) THE TREASURE-FINDER.

There was once a labouring-man who was working for another man by digging up his field.

Suddenly he had a joyful surprise. He discovered a treasure that had been hidden by someone in the ground. Perhaps this person had been afraid of being robbed of his treasure. He had hoped to come and dig it up later on, but had never had the chance. Perhaps he had died.

But how thrilled the labourer was by his wonderful discovery! He was determined to make the treasure his own. So he first hid it again in the ground so that no one should see it. Then he went to the owner of the field and said he wanted to buy the field.

But he found the price the owner asked was

more than he could pay. So he went and sold all that he had: house, furniture and everything else.

Then he took the money he got and bought the field and the treasure was his. And it was of far greater value than anything and everything he had given up for it.

So Jesus said: 'That is the sort of thing a man will do in order to belong to the Kingdom of God, when once he has seen the beauty of it.'

That is what the disciples did. They thought it such a glorious thing to become a disciple of Jesus that they joyfully gave up everything for it.

The second story Jesus told was called:

(5) 'THE PEARL OF GREAT PRICE.'

There was once a man who had a passion for lovely pearls. Whenever he heard of pearls being sold he went and examined them and bought all the very good ones.

He had been doing this for many years, so he had become an expert in knowing when pearls were really good ones.

As he found more and more perfect ones he sold the old ones and now he had a collection of very beautiful ones indeed. He was very proud of his lovely pearls. But he was never satisfied. He always hoped that he would find one more perfect than any he had yet seen.

Jesus approaches Jerusalem

One day he heard of another place where pearls were being sold, so he made the journey to see them. He found the pearls spread out for inspection and he took them in his hand one by one, holding them up to the light.

Suddenly his face lit up. In great excitement he picked out one pearl and taking it to the window he looked at it closely.

Yes, he was not mistaken. Here at last was the pearl he had been seeking all his life. He had found a perfect pearl!

But the price! It was very great indeed. How could he possibly pay for it? He had taken money with him but it was not nearly enough.

But he must have that pearl! He must be quick. So he hurried home, gathered together the whole of his collection of beautiful pearls of which he had been so proud, and sold the lot. Then he hurried back to the shop and with the money bought the perfect pearl. He was quite content, nay joyful, to let everything else go if only he might possess this treasure.

Well, Jesus said, that perfect pearl is like the Kingdom of God, and when anyone really understands what it is like, he joyfully gives up all his earthly treasures in order to possess it.

You see that is just what the rich young

o

man, who came to Jesus, would not do. Jesus told him he would have the best of all treasures, treasure in Heaven, if only he would give up his earthly treasure and follow Him. But he clung to his riches and let the Heavenly riches go.

It was as though the man in the story had clung to his collection of beautiful pearls and had let the one perfect pearl go. He would have been sorry all the rest of his life. And you remember the rich young man was sorrowful.

Jesus told the people that the best of all treasures is to have God with us, living in our hearts. And He began to talk to them once more about the great love of their Heavenly Father. He was never tired of talking about this because it was such a joy to Him. Jesus showed what this love was like when He made friends of all kinds of people. You will remember how those Pharisees were angry with Jesus because He made friends with sinful people. But Jesus said these people were 'lost', meaning the loving Father had not yet found them. But He was looking for them all the time.

Then Jesus told a story about this called:

(6) THE LOST SHEEP; AND THE LOST COIN.

Jesus saw a number of shepherds amongst

the crowd who were listening to Him and He said: 'You shepherds will understand this story very well.

There was a shepherd who had a hundred sheep. Each evening he gathered them into the fold, counting them as they passed in. Then he guarded them all night from the wild animals that prowled about after dark.

But one evening when he counted them he found there were only ninety-nine. One of them had strayed away from the rest of the flock.

Now he was a good shepherd and cared for his sheep. He cared for each one and he knew the name of the one that was lost. He knew it was in great danger. He was not content to have the ninety-nine. He must have that *lost* one.

So he got another shepherd to look after the ninety-nine and went after the one that was lost.

It was a lonely and dangerous journey. He carried a lantern with him and he listened as he went along for any sound that might lead him to his lost sheep.

The way was very rough and steep and sometimes he got badly scratched by thorns so that the blood flowed. He clambered down dangerous precipices and searched dark ravines; anywhere, everywhere he went looking for the sheep that was dear to him. He never thought of giving up.

At last he heard a cry. He followed the sound, flashing his lantern into all the dark corners. Then he saw something white and there was the lost sheep on a ledge part way down a precipice! It had not been able to climb either up or down.

The good shepherd, at great risk to himself, managed to reach the sheep and rescue it from its dangerous position.

Then how joyful he was! The sheep was too tired to walk so he laid it across his shoulders and carried it all the way back to the fold.

He was so happy that the next day he told his friends the whole story and said: "Isn't it grand that I found it, and it is now safe and sound?"

'Yes,' Jesus said, 'you shepherds would feel like that, wouldn't you?

And do you not think your Heavenly Father feels like that when one lost child of His is found? Yes, whenever a sinful child is sorry he has done wrong and begins to try to be good, your loving Father and all the angels in Heaven are filled with joy.'

Now some of the women who were listening to Jesus wore an ornamental band round their foreheads. It was hung with ten pieces of shining silver. They greatly valued these head ornaments. Probably Mary, the mother of Jesus, wore one.

So Jesus said to these women:

'What would you do if one of those silver pieces you prize so much came loose, rolled away, and got lost? Would you not light a lamp to look for it? And if you couldn't see it anywhere even then, would you not get a brush and sweep the whole house and go on hunting everywhere until you found it?

And how delighted you would be when at last you did find it! You would tell all your friends and neighbours and say: "Isn't it splendid that I have found the silver piece that I had lost?"

Well, God, your loving Father, is like that. He never ceases to seek for a lost child of His until He finds it. And when He has found it He is filled with joy, and the angels ring all the bells of Heaven.'

Then Jesus told this loveliest of all stories, which we call:

(7) THE PRODIGAL SON.

There was once a man who was a farmer and he had two sons working with him on the farm, as well as a number of farm-labourers.

One day the younger son came to his father and said: 'Father, before very long you will be dividing your property between my brother and myself. May I have my share now, please?'

So the father, being a kind-hearted man, divided all he had between his two sons.

The next day the younger son left his father and his home and travelled into a far country. And having no father now to control him, he soon got into bad company.

His gay friends were only too pleased to help him spend his money on wrong-doing, and when it was all finished they left him to manage as well as he could.

Then a worse thing happened. The crops failed and a great famine came to that far country. There was not enough food for any-one, so everything became very expensive. The boy's money was all spent and he was in great want.

He went to a farmer to beg for work that he might earn a little money to buy bread. The man had no work for him but he sent him into the fields to feed pigs. But he gave him nothing to eat before he went.

The boy was famished and faint with hunger and he would have been thankful even to have filled himself with the pig-food, but he was given nothing at all.

Then, at last, he began to think, and he said to himself: 'What a fool I've been! Why, my father's farm-labourers have more food given them than they can eat and here am I, his son, dying of hunger! I will go straight back home to my father and I will say to him: Father, I have been wicked before God and towards you. I am not fit to be called your son any more; make me one of your farm-labourers.'

So, just as he was, in his filthy rags and barefooted, he set out to tramp the long road home again.

Now the father had never ceased to miss his boy. And every day he had stood at the open door looking out in the hope of seeing him coming home.

So when the ragged boy was still a long way off, his father saw him coming. And his heart so leapt with joy that he ran all the way to meet him and threw his arms round him and kissed him over and over again.

Then the boy began the speech he had got ready to say to his father: 'Father, I have been wicked . . .' but his father cut it short and hurried the lad home.

Then he called out to his servants: 'Quick now, bring out that new suit! Strip him of these rags and put it on him. Put a ring on his finger and shoes on his feet. Now bring that fine fat calf; kill it and cook it. We will have a feast and a really good merry-making. I had lost this dear lad of mine and now he is found; he was dead to me but now he is alive again!'

So the music struck up and they began to be right merry, dancing and singing.

Now the elder son knew nothing at all about this because he had been busy in the field.

When he had finished his work he set out as usual for home and supper. But when he got near to the house he heard the sound of the music and dancing.

So he called one of the servants and said: 'What does all this mean?'

And the servant answered: 'Why, your brother has come back home and your father is so glad to have him safe and sound that he is having a feast and a merry-making. They have killed and cooked that fine fat calf.'

But the elder brother was angry and would not go in. Then his father came out and pleaded with him to come in and share in the rejoicing over his brother.

But he said: 'Look here, father, haven't I slaved for you all these years and never once disobeyed you in anything? Yet you have never even given me a kid that I might invite my friends and have a merry-making.

But as soon as this son of yours thinks fit to return home after squandering your money right and left, you meet him with open arms and even have the fine fat calf killed for him.'

But the father said: 'My boy, surely you belong to the home and you and I are always together. Does not all I have belong to you? It was only natural that we should make merry on a day like this. Your brother was dead to you but now he is alive again. You had lost your brother but now he is found!'

By this beautiful story Jesus wants to show us that the loving Heavenly Father welcomes His wandering children when they turn their faces homeward in just that way, and rejoices over them as that kind-hearted father did over his boy.

That was the way Jesus welcomed the publicans and sinners who came to Him, for He said: 'Whoever comes to Me, I will on no account cast him out.'

And those Pharisees who were angry with Jesus because of His love for these outcast people, were just like that angry elder brother, were they not?

Jesus once told these Pharisees a little story to show them how wrong it was to think themselves good and always in the right, and other people sinful and always in the wrong. We will call it:

(8) THE PHARISEE AND THE PUBLICAN.

Two men went into the Temple (or church)

to pray. One of them was a Pharisee and the other a publican.

The Pharisee stood and prayed like this with himself: 'O God, I thank Thee that I am not like other men. Some are cheats, some hard-hearted, some lead bad lives. I thank Thee I am not like these, nor like this publican here. I fast twice in the week and give away a tenth of all I earn.'

But the publican, feeling very humble before God, did not dare to come near to the altar, but stood afar off. And he would not so much as lift his eyes to Heaven, but beating his breast in sorrow for his sins said: 'God be merciful to me a sinner.'

'I tell you,' Jesus said, 'this publican's prayer was heard and he went home feeling God's smile resting upon him. But not so the Pharisee. For pride separates us from God, but meekness lifts us up into His presence.'

Afterwards Jesus said: 'If your Heavenly Father is so kind and forgiving to you, you ought to be the same to one another.'

And He taught His disciples to say in their prayers: 'Forgive us our trespasses (wrongdoings) as we forgive those that trespass against us.'

And He said: 'If you do not forgive those who do wrong to you, how can you expect your Heavenly Father to forgive you your wrong-doings?'

Then Peter said: 'Master, how often must I forgive my brother? If he wrongs me as many as seven times must I still forgive him?'

I think Jesus must have smiled at this question of Peter's. Then He said: 'Not seven times only, Peter, but seventy times seven!'

Jesus really meant by this that we must never count the number of times we forgive anyone, but just go on forgiving to the end, no matter how many times they hurt us.

Then Jesus told Peter this story to help him to understand. It is called:

(9) The Unforgiving Servant.

There was a certain king, who had a servant whose duty it was to look after the king's money and keep his accounts correctly. The king thought he would see how this man was doing his work.

So he looked through his account-books and he found that this servant had cheated him out of the huge sum of two million pounds. He had spent it on his own pleasures.

The king was very angry and commanded that this servant should be brought before him. This was done and the king said to him: 'If you do not pay this money at once you will be sold, also your wife, your children, your house and furniture and everything else you possess, and the money used to pay off some of your debt.'

The servant was terribly upset as he had spent all the money and had nothing to pay with.

So he fell down at the king's feet and cried out: 'O sir, only be patient and give me time and I will pay you all.'

The king had a kind heart and felt sorry for the man. And as he knew he could never pay this huge debt, he forgave him and crossed it off his account-book.

Of course the servant was very glad to have been let off, but he could have felt no gratitude to the kind king or he would never have acted as he did straightway afterwards.

Jesus said this man went outside and there he found another servant who owed him the small sum of five pounds.

What did this bad man do but seize this other poor servant by the throat and, shaking him, shout: 'Pay me what you owe me at once or it will be the worse for you!'

Well, the man had no money to pay just then, so he fell down and pleaded with him saying: 'Only be patient and give me time and I will pay you all.'

Now this was what the cruel servant had said to the king, wasn't it?

But he had already forgotten how good and merciful the king had been to him. He had the poor man dragged off to prison and said: 'There you lie until you have paid me all.'

Now the other servants of the king had seen all this and were highly indignant and disgusted. So they went to the king and told him what they had seen.

Then the king was very angry, and calling the cruel and unforgiving servant before him he said: 'You wicked man! I forgave you and crossed off your debt because you begged me to do so. Do you not see that you ought to have done the same? I had pity on you; why did you not have pity on your fellow-servant?'

Then the king in his anger had the cruel man cast into prison until he should pay his debt.

Then Jesus said: 'You see, you must be forgiving if you want God to forgive you.' We must remember this when we say the Lord's Prayer.

Jesus also taught us that we must always help anyone who has need of us.

One day a certain man came to Him and asked the same question that the rich young man had asked: 'Master, what shall I do that I may live forever with God in the Heavenly Home?'

Jesus said to him: 'Are you not one of

those who study and teach the Scriptures? Surely you ought to know! What does the Bible say you should do?'

'It says,' the man answered, 'thou shalt love the Lord thy God with all thy soul and with all thy strength and with all thy mind, and thy neighbour as thyself.'

Then Jesus said to him: 'You have answered rightly. Do this and you will live forever with God.'

But the man asked Jesus then: 'And who is my neighbour that I am to love as myself?'

Jesus answered the man by telling him this story. It is called:

(10) THE GOOD SAMARITAN.

There was once a man walking from Jerusalem to Jericho. The road he had to travel was known to be the haunt of brigands or robbers.

About half-way between Jerusalem and Jericho there was a deep gorge and along its sides were many dark caves where these robbers could hide. For this reason most people avoided this road if they could.

Well, when this traveller reached this dark gorge, sure enough out sprang a number of these robbers and set upon him.

Not satisfied with taking his money, they stripped the clothes from his back and when he struggled they knocked him about so un-mercifully that they left him lying half-dead by the roadside.

Now it happened that a certain priest was going down that way. Surely he will do some-thing for this poor man? But no! He gave a glance at him lying there, then passed by on the other side of the road.

Then a Levite came along to the place. He was supposed to be a good man because he helped in the Temple of God. But he just looked at the wounded man and then he also crossed the road and passed on his way.

But a certain Samaritan as he journeyed also came to where this poor man was lying. Now the priest and the Levite, being Jews, thought themselves much better than any Samaritan. But we shall see.

When this Samaritan saw the plight this wounded man was in, his heart was filled with pity. He got down from the donkey on which he was riding, knelt beside the poor man and bound up his wounds, pouring in oil and wine.

Then he very carefully lifted him on to the donkey and, walking himself beside the animal, brought the man to an inn.

Then he put him to bed, gave him nourish-ing drinks and sitting by him took care of him all through the night.

In the morning he slipped quietly from the

bedroom and finding the landlord of the inn gave him money and said: 'Take care of him for me. I shall be coming back this way in a few days and I will then call and repay you all you have spent on him.'

'Now,' said Jesus, 'which of these three do you think was neighbour to the man who was attacked by the robbers?'

The man answered: 'I suppose the one who was so kind to him.'

'Well then,' said Jesus, 'you go and do as he did.'

Jesus showed the man by this story that our neighbour is just anyone who needs our help.

A little while after this Jesus told another story about those who had been kind like the good Samaritan and those who had been unkind like the priest and the Levite. We will call it:

(11) THE STORY OF THE SHEEP AND THE GOATS.

Jesus had been talking about what we call the Judgment Day.

Jesus will be seated upon a throne like a king on that day. And before Him will stand everyone who has lived upon this earth.

Then He will separate the people one from another as a shepherd divides his sheep from the goats.

Jesus prays in the Garden of Gethsemane while His disciples sleep

And He will set the sheep, the good kind people, on His right hand, but the goats, the unkind ones, on His left.

Then Jesus, the King, will say to those on His right hand: 'Come, you happy ones; you are greatly loved of My Father. Come and live forever in the beautiful Home that has been ready for you from the time the world was made. For when I was hungry you gave Me food, when I was thirsty you gave Me drink, when I was a stranger you took Me in, when I was naked you clothed Me; I was sick and in prison and you visited Me.'

Then the kind people will be very much surprised and will say to Jesus: 'Lord, whenever did we see you hungry and give you food, or thirsty and give you drink, or a stranger and take you in? When did we see you naked and clothe you, or sick and in prison and visit you?'

Then Jesus, the King, will say: 'Because you did these things to anyone you saw in need, you did them to me. For all, even the very least, are My dear brothers and sisters.'

Then Jesus will say to those unkind ones on His left hand: 'You are shut out from the wonderful happiness of those who have been kind and loving because you have done nothing to deserve it. I was hungry and you gave Me no food, thirsty and you gave Me no

H

drink, naked and you did not clothe Me, a stranger and you turned Me away, sick and in prison and you never visited Me.'

Then these also will be surprised and will say: 'Lord, we cannot remember ever seeing you hungry or thirsty or naked, or a stranger, or sick and in prison, so how could we help you?'

Then Jesus will say: 'Because you did not do it even to one of the least of My brothers and sisters in need you did it not to Me.'

Then those who have been kind and unselfish will be happy forever in the Heavenly Home. But the selfish and unkind will be turned away and will be very sad to think of all they have missed.

Now Jesus told other stories also, which you may read for yourselves. As you grow older you will understand them all much better than you do now.

CHAPTER XII

JESUS RIDES INTO JERUSALEM

There are those who live well together following the Good Shepherd, and those who live for themselves. Jesus showed these the better way, but they set their heart against Him, and *plotted* against Him. They didn't want a Good Shepherd, but a king who would drive out their enemies, the Romans, by force.

Also they wanted to win the praise of men; they were hypocrites—their religion was an outward show, following a set of rules which pressed like a burden on common people; they even wanted to stop Him healing and helping on the Sabbath day, but He said: 'You would help one of your sheep out of a pit on the Sabbath day, wouldn't you?' And He taught all willing to learn, rich or poor, that the more we love God the more we find to love in others.

Many of those who set their heart against Him and plotted to get rid of Him lived in Jerusalem. He knew His Father wanted Him to meet them and tell them what the Father really wanted from those who call themselves His worshippers.

He decided to go there, whatever the cost. How brave He was! He told His disciples what sufferings awaited Him there. They tried, especially Peter, to stop Him. Jesus said: 'You are not helping Me, only hindering God's work.' Thomas was frightened, but tried to be brave for Jesus's sake, saying, 'Let us also go that we may die with Him.'

So Jesus travelled on to Jerusalem, doing good; speaking beautiful and wonderful words and healing the sick all along the way as He went. And crowds of people followed Him. He had a long way to go.

Many of these people believed that Jesus was the Messiah, the Son of God. This made the enemies of Jesus more angry than ever. But Jesus went quietly and bravely on His way.

Now, just at the time when Jesus was drawing near to Jerusalem, a great festival was being held there. It was the same one Joseph and Mary had gone to every year, and Jesus also, for the first time, when He was twelve years old. You remember it was called The Feast of the Passover.

Crowds of people had come from all over the country and from lands afar off. Most of these people had come to worship God in the beautiful Temple and to offer gifts there.

When Jesus was quite near to Jerusalem

He said to two of His disciples: 'Go into that little village over there and as soon as you enter it you will see a donkey tied to a door and a colt with her. Untie the colt and bring it to Me. And if anyone says to you: "Why are you untying that young donkey?" you must answer: "Because the Lord needs him," and at once the owner of the colt will allow you to take him.'

So the two disciples went and they found everything just as Jesus said they would. The owner must have been a friend of Jesus, must he not?

When they had brought the colt to Jesus they spread their cloaks on its back for Him to sit upon. For Jesus was about to ride into Jerusalem like a king, the King of the Jews, if they would only have Him.

You may think it strange then, that when He was about to ride in state, He should ride on a donkey.

But in that country donkeys were very fine animals and cost a lot of money. Many were white in colour and looked very beautiful. All the important people rode on these donkeys. It was only the soldiers who rode on horses.

So Jesus rode, not as a soldier-king at the head of an army sitting on a horse, but as the Prince of Peace, sitting on an ass.

Perhaps Jesus wanted to give those hard-hearted enemies of His in Jerusalem a last chance to receive Him as their King, the Messiah whom God had sent to them from Heaven. He loved them although they hated Him.

So Jesus rode over the Mount of Olives. And when He saw the city he loved so much with its beautiful white marble Temple, golden roof and dome shining in the sun, He wept over it.

For Jesus knew that a very dreadful time was coming for Jerusalem, when its enemies would surround it on every side. They would cast down that beautiful Temple and not leave one stone in the city standing upon another. And as the tears ran down His cheeks Jesus cried out: 'O Jerusalem, Jerusalem, you who have killed the prophets and stoned to death those My Father has sent to you, how often would I have gathered your children together as a hen gathers her chickens under her wings, but you would not let Me.'

Then Jesus rode down the slope of the mountain with the disciples and a crowd of people who loved Him. And those who loved Him and were looking out for Him in Jerusalem, saw the crowd coming and Jesus riding in the midst.

Then they cried out: 'He is coming, our

King, our Messiah!' and they went out quickly to meet Him, singing and shouting for joy as they went.

By the roadside palm-trees were growing and as the people passed they broke off branches and waved them joyously. It was the custom in that country to wave palms to show joy.

Many children were in the crowd that went out to meet Jesus. All children loved Jesus, and we know how much He loved them. He had taken them in His arms and blessed them more than once.

So now they sang and shouted with the rest to welcome the Messiah as He rode into the city. They waved their palm branches and strewed the silvery fronds upon the ground for Jesus to ride upon. Some people also to show their love, threw down their cloaks.

So Jesus rode through the gate into Jerusalem and then went up to the Temple He so much loved. And all the people gathered in the city for the festival were astonished to see and hear this joyful entry of Jesus, with the people singing, shouting and praising Him.

But those men who hated Jesus were watching all this and they said to Him: 'Do you not hear what these people are saying about you? Why don't you stop them saying these things and making all this fuss?'

For these men did not believe that Jesus was the Messiah and the Son of God.

But Jesus said to them: 'If these people and these little children were not singing praises to God, the very stones would cry out. Do you not know and have you nor read that God has taught little children to praise Him best of all?'

Then Jesus did another brave thing, something He knew would anger His enemies more than ever.

I told you those who came to the festival to worship God offered gifts in the Temple. Those who had enough money to buy it, gave an ox or a sheep to God, but poorer people gave a dove or a pigeon.

Now these things were sold in the outer courts of the Temple and some of the men who sold them were not very honest. Other men had to arrange for receiving the money and many of them cheated the worshippers who bought from them.

Now you remember how much Jesus loved the beautiful Temple when He was a boy, because it was the House of His Heavenly Father. Well, He loved it even more now, so that the love He had for it was like a fire burning in His heart.

You can imagine, then, how Jesus would hate to see all this wickedness going on in the courts of the holy Temple. Jesus was angry sometimes, and His anger was so great now that He made a whip of thin cords and drove out the sheep and oxen before Him.

Then He strode over to those men who cheated the worshippers out of their money and poured out the coins they had taken and turned their tables upside down. And He said to them: 'It is written in the Bible, "My House shall be called a House of Prayer", but you have made it a den of robbers.'

Then He went to those who were selling pigeons and doves and said: 'Take those things out at once. Don't make My Father's House into a shop.'

So you see Jesus could be stern when it was needed. Afterwards, when everything was quiet, Jesus talked to the people in the Temple and told them His beautiful stories.

But His enemies wanted more than ever to kill Him and could not find any way of taking Him because He was constantly surrounded by crowds of people, eagerly listening to every word He said.

Now in the Temple there was a box into which people who came to worship dropped money for the poor.

Jesus, looking up, saw the rich men dropping in large coins.

Then He saw a poor widow woman come

along and drop into the box two mites. A mite was the smallest piece of money there was in that country, only worth about half a farthing.

But Jesus knew how very poor this widow was and that it was very likely she would have to go without a meal in order to give those two mites. So Jesus said: 'I tell you truly, this poor widow has dropped in more than any of the rich men did. For they have so much that they will never miss what they have given. But she has given her very last copper.'

Every day during the festival Jesus came to the Temple and spoke to the people. And every night He left the city and slept at a friend's house on the Mount of Olives. And every morning, very early, crowds of people came to the Temple to listen to Him.

But all the time His enemies went on plotting, plotting how they might put Him to death.

Chapter XIII

HOW JESUS 'LOVED THEM TO THE END'

(1) The Last Supper.

Judas, the man from Kerioth (we say Judas Iscariot), one of the Twelve, was like a treasurer, in charge of their money; but he learned to love the money itself, and to take some for himself. He actually agreed to accept 30 pieces of silver from the enemies of Jesus, and for that sum to betray Him.

Jesus had a very great longing to have a last supper with his twelve disciples before He left this world. So Peter and John found a large supper room in the house of a friend of Jesus, and there they prepared the meal.

It was during this supper that Jesus rose from the table and washed the disciples' feet (John 13).

After that He became very sad and troubled, and said: 'One of you will betray Me to My enemies.'

They all began to say: 'Lord, is it I? Is it I?'

John, with his head leaning on the breast of Jesus, said: 'Lord, who is it?'

Judas said: 'Surely it isn't me?'

Jesus said to him: 'Is it not?' and, to show He knew as well as Judas, handed him a piece of bread dipped in the soup (usually meant as a special favour). And Judas at once rose from the table and went out into the night.

Then Jesus took a loaf of bread in His hands, and, breaking it He gave a piece to each of His disciples.

Then He took a large cup of wine that was on the table and passed it round for each one to drink.

And He said: 'When I am gone away from you, do this together. And as you drink the cup think of My blood that is shed for you. Do this, after I am gone, in memory of Me.'

Then Jesus added: 'This one thing I ask you to do. Love one another, as I have loved you. When people see you loving one another, they will know you are My disciples.'

(2) JESUS IN GETHSEMANE—BETRAYED.

Jesus and His disciples had been seated on a slope of the Mount of Olives while He had been saying some of these beautiful things. He led them over a little brook to a favourite spot called the Garden of Gethsemane.

Judas, too, knew it well.

Jesus began to be very sorrowful indeed.

He turned to His Heavenly Father as always. He said to His disciples: 'You sit here while I go over yonder and pray.'

But He took with Him Peter and James and John—'for company' in His great sorrow and suffering, saying: 'Stay here and watch with Me' as if to say: 'I have always given you My sympathy. I need yours now.'

Then He went a little further into the shadows and, falling on His face, He cried out: 'O My Father, if it be possible save Me from the terrible suffering that is coming to Me, but, nevertheless, do not let what I wish be done, unless it is what You, My Father, also wish.'

Jesus prayed so, again and again.

The Three went to sleep, even then. But He excused them, kind and gentle, even then, as always.

If only they had kept awake they would have heard His voice, quite calm now—'I come to do Thy will'—surer than ever of His Father's love.

Come let us sing of a wonderful love,
    Tender and true;
Out of the heart of the Father above,
    Streaming to me and to you:
      Wonderful love
Dwells in the heart of the Father above.

Jesus, the Saviour, this good news to tell,
    Joyfully came;
Came with the helpless and hopeless to dwell,
    Sharing their sorrow and shame;
       Seeking the lost,
Saving, redeeming at measureless cost.

Jesus's calm was broken by the sound of stealthy footsteps. He must not let the Three be caught and perhaps killed.

Quickly, yet gently, He said: 'Get up quickly; let us be going; the one who is betraying Me to My enemies is close at hand.'

Judas and the band of soldiers appeared, with torches and lanterns (it was still dark) and weapons in their hands.

Judas had said: 'Take the one I kiss; that is the one.' So he did, saying: 'Hail, rabbi!' with a kiss.

Jesus said: 'Friend, do your errand.'

And to the soldiers: 'Who is it you are looking for?'

'Jesus of Nazareth.'

'I am He,' Jesus said, so calmly that the soldiers fell back and dropped to the ground in fear of Him.

Once again the same question from Him, and from them the same answer.

Then Jesus, still guarding His disciples, said: 'It's Me you want; let these get away.' He not only loved them *to the end* (John 13[1]), but needed them to carry on the work He had begun (Acts 1[1]) *afterwards*.

Peter, wanting to defend Him, drew his sword and cut the ear of one man.

Jesus said: 'Put away your sword, Peter; if My Father thinks it for the best that I should suffer, shall I not be willing?'

When the soldiers seized Jesus, the disciples fled, leaving Him . . . alone? No. His great Friend never left Him.

(3) THE TRIAL.

The soldiers led Jesus to the court of the High Priest, who really had no right to try Him, but was set on His death.

Jesus's enemies at first could not find true witnesses. Jesus was silent. The High Priest knew that did not mean 'guilty', so accused Him of posing as the 'Messiah'. Then Jesus said bravely 'Yes.' By that He boldly declared Himself the 'Son of God'. The priests called that 'blasphemy' or speaking evil against God Himself, a crime worthy of death.

The High Priest could not order His death, so he sent Him for trial to Pilate the Roman Governor.

You may read how Peter, as brave as he then could be, went on following his Master, but at a 'safe' distance. How in a room near the court he denied Jesus with a curse when a servant-maid taunted him with being a follower of Jesus and with speaking like a fisherman from Galilee; how Jesus, passing just then, looked at him with a look that nearly broke his heart; how Pilate, not knowing what 'Messiah' really meant, could find no fault in Jesus.

Indeed, Pilate could not help seeing Jesus was truly like a king in bearing, in character, in courage, and asked Him: 'You *are* a King then?'

'Yes,' said Jesus, 'I was born to be a King, but not of this world.'

This answer cleared Jesus completely from the charge that He had been stirring up a rebellion against the Roman government. That encouraged Pilate to pronounce Him innocent.

'Crucify Him! crucify Him!' yelled the crowd.

Pilate did try hard to get Jesus off, but at last the crowd cried out: 'This man has plotted to set Himself up as a king, so He is a traitor to Caesar, the Emperor! So if you set Him free you are no friend of Caesar's.'

Then Pilate, afraid of offending Caesar, who could sack him in a moment, tried again and said: 'Shall I crucify your King?'

The crowd answered at once: 'We have no king but Caesar.'

That was another threat to Pilate. He gave way to fear, and handed Jesus over to them to be crucified.

Outwardly, he 'washed his hands' from the blood of Jesus. But inwardly he was a coward.

And what of Judas? Perhaps he hoped to the last that he could make Jesus accept the position of 'king', *his* kind of 'king', and use force against the Romans. But now, seeing what he had done, and done to his best friend —full of bitter grief and remorse, he went out and put himself to death.

(4) THE CRUCIFIXION.

There is a green hill far away,
    Without a city wall,
Where the dear Lord was crucified
    Who died to save us all.

We may not know, we cannot tell
    What pains He had to bear;
But we believe it was for us
    He hung and suffered there.

He died that we might be forgiven,
    He died to make us good,
That we might go at last to heaven,
    Saved by His precious blood.

I

Why do we sing ' . . . In England's green and pleasant land'?

Well, it isn't *all* green, nor all pleasant; but when we are across the water, especially in dry climates, and see near us brown parched land, we do see in our mind 'a green and pleasant land'.

And when we think of our dear Lord, bright and brave, tender and true, sharing sorrow and shame, seeking the lost, saving, redeeming at measureless cost, the place where He gave His life and gave pardon to a penitent thief turning to Him will always be green in our memory. And when we see 'sorrow and love flow mingled down', we shall want to bring to Him our tribute, a life ever green with love, growing like His.

> Love so amazing, so divine,
> Demands my soul, my life, my all.

CHAPTER XIV

THE MOST WONDERFUL STORY
OF ALL

THE saddest people in all the world then were the eleven disciples. They were gathered together in a large upper room with others who loved Jesus.

They were terribly disappointed. They said to one another sorrowfully: 'We thought He was the Messiah, the Son of God, but how could that be when He could not save himself from being put to death?'

They had quite forgotten what Jesus had once said: 'No one can take My life from Me. I lay it down of Myself. I have power to lay it down and I have power to take it up again. This power I have received from My Father.'

Jesus was crucified and was laid in the tomb on the day we now call Good Friday. He lay there all day on Saturday.

On Sunday morning, very early, Mary Magdalene came to the tomb. She and a few other women who loved Jesus had brought spices and ointment to anoint His body, as was the custom in that country. They were wondering who they could get to help them to roll away that great stone so that they could enter the tomb.

But to their amazement they found the stone had already been rolled away and the tomb was open.

Mary at once thought that the body of Jesus had been stolen during the night and she ran with all speed to the house where Peter and John were and cried out: 'Someone has taken the Lord out of the tomb and we don't know where they have laid Him.'

Peter and John were as full of amazement as the women had been, and they at once left the house and set off towards the tomb.

As they got nearer they both began to run, and John outran Peter and got to the tomb first.

He found things exactly as the women had said. The tomb was open. It was like a cave, you know, and John stooped down and looked in. He saw the linen cloths that had been wrapped round the body of Jesus, lying there, but Jesus was gone.

Then Peter reached the tomb and, in his impulsive way, went straight in. He also saw the linen cloths lying there and the napkin that had been folded round the head of Jesus, not just thrown with the other cloths, but lying, still folded where His head had been.

Then John went into the tomb also and when he saw how the linen cloths were lying and the body of Jesus gone, the truth suddenly flashed upon him. Then he remembered what all the disciples seemed, strangely enough, to have forgotten, that Jesus had said *He would rise again on the third day*. This was the third day! There could be no mistake about it. Jesus had risen; He was alive again! John ran along with Peter to tell the marvellous news to the other disciples.

But Mary still lingered there. She hadn't seen what Peter and John had seen. It was strange they didn't tell her what they had found out, but I suppose they were so excited that they just dashed away and forgot poor Mary.

There she stood weeping outside the tomb, longing to know where the body of Jesus had been taken.

Then turning round she saw Someone standing near to her. She thought it was the gardener, for the tomb was in a garden. Then He spoke. He said: 'My woman, why are you weeping?'

Mary answered: 'Oh sir, if you are the one who has carried the body of Jesus away, only tell me where you have laid Him and I will go and take Him away.'

Then the One who was standing there just said: 'Mary!'

She knew that voice! Only One could say 'Mary' in that tone.

'Master!' she gasped.

Then Jesus said to her: 'Mary, go and tell My brethren, all My disciples and those who love Me, that very soon I shall leave this world and ascend to My Father, where I was before I came. I shall now go into Galilee and I will see them there.'

Now Galilee, if you remember, was the place where Jesus had called most of the disciples to follow Him and where they had had such happy times together.

You can imagine how quickly and eagerly Mary would go to give that message to the disciples. She came rushing into the room crying: 'I have seen the Lord!'

And when they saw the happiness in her face, the face that only a few hours before had been so sad, they felt that her words were true.

How Jesus showed Himself to Thomas and Peter you may read in John 20$^{19\text{-}29}$ and in John 21$^{1\text{-}23}$.

Now on the very day Jesus rose from the dead (Easter Sunday we now call it), He showed Himself alive to two other people who loved Him.

These two were walking from Jerusalem to a village called Emmaus, where they lived. It was a walk of about seven miles.

They had been in Jerusalem when Jesus was crucified and they were now in great sorrow. As they walked along they were talking together about it all.

Then Someone who had been walking along the road behind them caught them up and walking beside them spoke to them. It was Jesus, alive again, but they didn't know Him.

He said to them: 'What is it that you are talking about as you walk and look so sad?'

Then they stood still and one of them, called Cleopas, said: 'You must be a stranger living all by yourself in Jerusalem not to have heard of the things that have been happening there.'

'What things?' He asked them.

'Why, the things about Jesus of Nazareth,' they replied. 'He both said and did very great and wonderful things before God and all the people. Did you not hear how the chief priests and our rulers gave Him up to be condemned to death and crucified him?

But we had hoped that He was the Messiah the Son of God, our Saviour. Alas! He is dead and this is the third day He has lain in the tomb.

But this morning we were greatly amazed by what certain women told us. They went very early this morning to the tomb and they said they found it open, the stone rolled away, and the body of Jesus gone. They also said they had seen in a vision, shining angels who told them Jesus was alive. And some of those who were with us went to the tomb and found what the women had said was quite true; the tomb was open but they had no sight of Jesus.'

Then He said to them: 'What foolish ones you are not to belive all that those great and good men, the prophets, have written all through the Bible about the Messiah! Do you not understand that it was right for the Messiah to suffer these things and then to be crowned with glory?'

Then He started at the beginning of the Bible and went all through, explaining to them everything that had been written about Himself.

By this time they were approaching the village where they were going. And He looked as though He intended to go further on. But they said to Him: 'Do come in and stay with us; it is late evening now and darkness will soon come upon you. Do come in!'

So He went in to stay the night with them and they asked Him to have supper with them. He sat down at the table and then He took the loaf of bread in His hands and said a blessing over it.

Then He broke it and gave a piece to each of them, *and at once they knew Him*! They had seen Him break bread in just that way so many times before. Yes, it was indeed Jesus their Lord! But as soon as they knew Him, He vanished out of their sight.

But how full of joy they were to know Jesus was really alive!

'Oh,' they cried, 'didn't our hearts glow within us as He talked to us by the way! How wonderfully He explained to us all that was written about Himself in the Bible! Now we understand. Come, let us go at once and tell the others all about it.'

Later, Jesus talked to many of the disciples gathered together. He told them He was trusting them to carry on the great work He had begun and for which He had been crucified. He said to them: 'Go into all the world and tell the Good News to everyone. Teach them, as I have taught you, what they must do to enter the Kingdom of Heaven and become children of the Heavenly Father.

You have been with Me all along. You have heard all that I have said and seen all that I have done, so you must be My witnesses. You must tell it all to everyone in the world, to all nations and peoples.

My Father has promised to send His Holy Spirit down upon each of you. Stay here until that happens. For after you have received the Spirit you will be able to do all these things; you will have the power to do them given to you. And remember, I am with you always and with all My loved ones, until the very end of the world.'

Then Jesus was received up into Heaven and sat down by the side of His loving Father.

And the disciples returned to Jerusalem with great joy. And they were constantly in the Temple praising and blessing God.

Then they set out as Jesus had bid them, telling the Good News everywhere. And Jesus worked with them wherever they went. For though they could not now see Him, they knew He was always with them as He is always with us. And He gave them power to heal the sick and the lame, and to cast out evil spirits from people's hearts. And very many people learned to love Jesus and became His disciples through their teaching.

And the great work is still going on, girls and boys, and will go on until the whole world is brought to God. You and I must help to bring in that glorious time!

It is a thing most wonderful,
  Almost too wonderful to be,
That God's own Son should come from heaven,
  And die to save a child like me.

And yet I know that it is true;
  He chose a poor and humble lot,
And wept and toiled and mourned and died,
  For love of those who loved Him not.

But even could I see Him die,
  I could but see a little part
Of that great love which like a fire
  Is always burning in His heart.